DUDLEY PUBLIC LIBRARIES

The loan of this book may be renewed if not required by other
readers, by contacting the library from which it was borrowed.

0145

You are going to enjoy this: a life of adventure – surviving the war years on the far side of the world, sailing, climbing, ski mountaineering, in many different parts of the world. It is inspiring that a Reverend should stick his neck out in this way – battling Atlantic storms, losing a mast in Antarctica, sailing continually in the Arctic, making the first ascents of mountains, skiing across remote regions, climbing with world class climbers, and sailing through the North West Passage. As a Commando, Bob is clearly made of the right stuff!

BEAR GRYLLS

ADDICTED TO ADVENTURE

BETWEEN ROCKS AND COLD PLACES

BOB SHEPTON

ADLARD COLES NAUTICAL

B L O O M S B U R Y

LONDON · NEW DELHI · NEW YORK · SYDNEY

For our youngest daughter Rachel,
who has faced real challenges in life and is winning

Adlard Coles Nautical
An imprint of Bloomsbury Publishing Plc

50 Bedford Square   1385 Broadway
London   New York
WC1B 3DP   NY 10018
UK   USA

www.bloomsbury.com

ADLARD COLES, ADLARD COLES NAUTICAL and the Buoy logo are trademarks of
Bloomsbury Publishing Plc

First published 2014
This edition published 2015

© Bob Shepton, 2014
Maps © John Plumer

British Library Cataloguing-in-Publication Data
A catalogue record for this book is available from the British Library.

Library of Congress Cataloguing-in-Publication data has been applied for.

ISBN: PB: 978-1-4729-0587-1
ePDF: 978-1-4729-0588-8
ePub: 978-1-4729-0589-5

CONTENTS

FOREWORD
BY SIR RANULPH FIENNES

This is the uniquely interesting and colourful life of an Anglican clergyman turned adventurer. It all started way back in pursuit of his ministry as part of the pastoral outreach and care with young people, especially when he was chaplain at two specialist schools. Bob never retired and his adventures covered the world.

So were they just the ordinary type of adventurous trip here and there? No not really, when you consider they encompass sailing to the Azores as a first ocean passage with school boys – not necessarily too taxing, although all navigation was done by sextant in those days – and then to Antarctica (losing the mast in the process), round Cape Horn, to the Arctic (including losing a boat to fire when wintering alone in the ice), to Alaska, and crossing the Atlantic fourteen times (so far) and never by the easy route, Canaries to the Caribbean. And finally there is the Northwest Passage in a comparatively small fibreglass boat.

So is it all sailing? By no means! There were those undiscovered and unclimbed cliffs and new rock routes in the 1960s and 1970s at Lulworth and Portland, which he set about developing with members of his church youth group – rumour has it that sometimes he had his climbing gear on ready under his clergy robes. Then new routes on the Ormes at Llandudno with boys from St David's College where he was chaplain, not without some amusing near disasters. And the first ascents of mountains and new rock climbs in Arctic Greenland and

Canada from the boat (sometimes literally stepping off the boat to start the climb), including climbing a new extreme route with 'world-class climbers' in Greenland in 2010 when 'of a certain age', for which expedition the whole group were each awarded a Piolet d'Or, perhaps the most prestigious award in the mountaineering world.

And skiing and ski mountaineering? Lots of that too, including ski instructing in Scotland and on the Continent, which included teaching British army groups in Bavaria for several years, downhill and touring, to earn money for the next expedition, sometimes living in extreme conditions to avoid the huge fees for accommodation in Switzerland for instance. Ski mountaineering in the Arctic yielded more first ascents of mountains, and included a repeat of the north-south traverse across Bylot Island in Arctic Canada by that well-known, enigmatic mountaineer and sailor of yesteryear, Bill Tilman.

Parachuting? Yes, but only to take boys from Kingham Hill School when he was chaplain there – 'probably the most scary thing I have done, but then I did start rather late in life for that sort of thing'. The formative years of his youth, especially his service with the Royal Marines, coupled with a resolute Christian life fitted him well for leadership and daring. This is a wonderful true tale of adventure with a wide variety of people of all ages, in different parts of the world and over many years. A long, full and varied life, stretching from the days of the British Empire to the present day. A truly interesting book which I definitely recommend.

FOREWORD
BY SIR CHRIS BONINGTON

Bob has climbed for most of his long life. Originally trained as a Cliff Leader in the Royal Marines, he was responsible for discovering and developing the limestone cliffs of Lulworth and Portland and bringing them to the attention of climbers. He made a number of first ascents of climbs on the Great and Little Ormes at Llandudno, with schoolboys, again in the early days of development.

In recent years he has led several private expeditions sailing to and climbing in Greenland and Arctic Canada, and his expeditions there have made over sixty first ascents of mountains and rock faces, not all of them technically hard, but a number also in the Extreme category, and all previously unclimbed. The members of his 'Greenland Big Wall Climbing Expedition' were awarded the Piolet d'Or in 2011, including Bob, and he has been called 'the modern Tilman'. All this as well as being, and often in conjunction with being, a Reverend.

It's an interesting and varied life; I commend it to you.

ARGENTINA

Río Gallegos

M a r

A r g e n t i n o

Falkland Islands
[U.K.]

Stanley

San Carlos

West
Falkland

East
Falkland

*Beauchene
Island*

A T L A N T I C

O C E A N

Río Grande

*Isla Grande
de
Tierra del Fuego*

Ushuaia

Islas de los Estados

Cape Horn

p a s s a g e

SOUTH
AMERICA

ANTARCTICA

Antarctic
Peninsula

Scotia Sea
Drak
PACIFIC
OCEAN
South Shetland Islands
Elephant Island
Clarence Island
Gibbs Island
King George Island
Maxwell Bay
Robert I.
Greenwich I.
Arturo Prat
Livingstone Island
Smith Island
Deception Island
Whalers Bay
Bransfield Strait
d'Urville Island
Joinville Island
Dundee Island
Low Island
Trinity Island
Palmer Archipelago
Trinity Peninsula
Cape Herschel
Erebus and Terror Gulf
James Ross Island
Snow Hill Island
Brabant Island
Gerlache Strait
Land
Anvers Island
Hughes Bay
Foyn Harbour
Neumayer Channel
Dorian Bay
Port Lockroy
Weddell Sea
Robertson Island
Graham
Vernadsky (Faraday)
Renaud Island
200nm

PROLOGUE

FIRE DOWN BELOW!

By Red Flower Bagheera meant fire, only no creature in the jungle
will call fire by its proper name. Every beast lives in deadly fear of it…
THE JUNGLE BOOK, RUDYARD KIPLING

It was during the winter of 2004/5 while alone, ice-bound in Greenland, that I made the simple mistake that destroyed my 33-foot Westerly sailing yacht *Dodo's Delight* and might well have cost me my life.

But sailing up a fjord in Greenland one month and skiing down the same fjord on the winter ice a month later had already been such an enjoyable, novel and intriguing experience.

The autumn had been brutal. A gale drove me out of my first anchorage. I had to haul in 40 metres of chain, hand over hand, as *Dodo* was blown fast across the fjord towards the rocky shore. My next anchorage, in a cove within a cove, was certainly better protected from southerly gales, but by a curious freak of tidal currents, when the winds were constantly in the north, ice floes would sneak around the corner from the nearby Upernavik Isfjord. A massive, borrowed warp I stretched across the entrance worked to keep fresh floes out, but it also entrapped the ice already inside the cove. When gales broke up the still-forming winter pack ice, huge sheets of it, scraped along *Dodo*'s sides. The noise was alarming, but at least at that early stage the ice was still soft and thin and did no real harm.

Eventually, once we were properly iced in, life became so much better. We were secure, protected by the ice sheet (pack ice); growlers and bergy bits or wind-driven floes could no longer reach us. The weather improved and my quality of life improved with it. Now I was able to get out on the ice and walk around, and I could ski over to the nearby settlement at Upernavik for fuel and stores.

Bringing fresh water aboard was much easier too, although it did remain a challenge. Simply getting from the tidal ice to the fast ice (sea ice 'locked' to the land) could be tricky and once, picking my way back to the boat, I stepped on to what I hoped was a solid shard between the fast and the tidal ice only for it to capsize and plunge me into freezing water. It was a struggle to lever myself out, but I managed it, shivering with cold, and was relieved to get back aboard to defrost and change my sodden clothes.

On land, snow shoes were essential footwear when dragging my sled with the water containers to and from the small fresh-water pool I had found, where a stream came down to near the water's edge. Knowing how radically the landscape would change as winter progressed and the heavy snows set in, I had thrust a ski into the ground to mark my precious water supply.

Even at first, in early winter, drawing water involved a good deal of digging, cutting out the snow in blocks in order to reach down and break the thin layer of ice covering the pool. After filling my containers I would stack all the cut blocks back in place then plug every crack with loose snow to stop the pool from freezing solid. Snow is a good insulator; on the boat, for example, I had deliberately let earlier falls pile up on the decks.

Skiing across the fjords one day I passed my first anchorage. I could see folds and fissures in the ice where *Dodo* had been; it was perhaps as well that I had been driven out by the gale.

The Arctic winter's constant darkness had begun to ease a little, although by the time I returned to the boat daylight was fading. After a cup of coffee and a bite to eat I took the portable generator up to the cockpit to charge the batteries. 'Must fill the diesel heater', I thought. I took the fuel container and a funnel along the deck, opened up the hole I had made in the deckhead, inserted the funnel and started to pour the diesel – it was a routine job that I had been doing for months.

Almost instantly red flames erupted from below. I had forgotten to put the other funnel under the deckhead. Instead of filling the header tank, diesel was spilling on to the stove's naked flame. The speed of it all was terrifying. I rushed to the main hatch, pushed it open and started down to fight the blaze. One breath and I knew instinctively that it would be fatal. The smoke and fumes were already too noxious.

After that it all became ridiculous. In a frantic attempt to extinguish the inferno I began scraping snow into a bucket and throwing it on the flames. It was pointless: snow contains comparatively little water, yet I fought on when I should have been throwing flammable gear such as gas cylinders off the boat. Had I not been so fixated on dousing the fire I could have saved more. Eventually, driven off the boat, I could do nothing but stand and watch while the conflagration consumed *Dodo* and all my possessions.

Alerted by someone who had seen the plume of black smoke from the airport on the hill above Upernavik, the local 'fire service' arrived on skidoos, but by then it was far too late to fight the blaze and their chief concern was to get me away from danger. I was put on the back of a skidoo and taken to Upernavik. Next day, all that was visible of my boat was a third of her mast sticking up out of the ice and, strewn around, a few forlorn fenders and gas bottles. Maybe I could have ducked under the smoke, perhaps wrapped a towel around my head. Maybe. Maybe I would have choked to death. I will never know.

Now, I had only the clothes I was standing up in – no money, no credit cards, no passport. The authorities came to my rescue. The police wrote a letter in Danish and English explaining the loss of my passport, and my wife Kate transferred funds to pay my airfare home from Greenland.

Would this be the end to adventuring? Well, we had best go right back to how it all began…

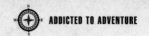

TIMELINE

1935	Born Batu Gajah, Malaya
1941	Sent to Australia with my sister Rosamond
1943	Back to Great Britain, mother, sister and myself. Pacific, Atlantic, U boats
1948	Bradfield College, Berkshire
1953–1955	Royal Marines, 45 and 42 Commando RM, Cliff Leader Course
1955–1958	Jesus College, Cambridge
1958–1959	Mayflower Family Centre, Canning Town, London
1959–1961	Oak Hill Theological College, Southgate, London
1961–1963	Curate, St John's Church, Weymouth
1963–1966	Boys' Club Leader, Cambridge University Mission, Bermondsey, London
1966–1969	Warden, Oxford Kilburn Club, Kilburn, London
1969–1977	Chaplain and Outdoor Pursuits Master, St David's College, Llandudno
1977–1980	Chief Instructor, Carnoch Outdoor Centre, Glencoe
1980–1992	Chaplain, Kingham Hill School, Kingham
1992	Retired

CHRONOLOGY OF VOYAGES

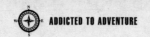
2008   Scotland – Horta – Ponta Delgado – Scotland (Azores
               – last visit, page 30)
               Delivery Flensburg – Antwerp – Curaçao – Panama –
               Peru
2009   Scotland – Paamiut – Akuliarusinguaq –
               Northumberland Island – Smith Sound – Aasiaat
               (Paradise regained, or at least revisited, page 151)
               Delivery UK – Las Palmas
2010   Aasiaat – Sortehul, Upernavik – Cape Farewell area
               – Prinz Christian Sund – Atlantic (*Impossible Wall*,
               Greenland: World-class climbers, page 164)
2012   Scotland – Paamiut – Upernavik – Pond Inlet –
               Resolute – Cambridge Bay – Tuktoyaktuk – Point
               Barrow – Bering Strait – Nome (The Northwest
               Passage, page 180)

01

ORIGINS

We ourselves feel that what we are doing is a drop in the ocean.
But the ocean would be less because of that missing drop.
MOTHER TERESA

AN INTERESTING LIFE?

I was born in 1935 in Batu Gajah, Malaya – now Malaysia, although
then a British colony – where my father managed a rubber plantation
some twenty miles from Kuantan on the east coast. Memories of
my early childhood remain vivid to this day: sitting on my father's
shoulders one evening, surveying the perimeter of the estate; 'coolies'
rushing from the factory shed to stop me from poking a stick at a cobra
coiled on the road; diagonal grooves cut in the rubber trees, dripping
latex sap into a cup set low on their trunks. And I have flashbacks of
our house, inside and out, and of my dear Amah, a sort of Chinese
nanny, who looked after me.

I was only six when, together with my twelve-year-old sister Rosamond, I was sent by plane to stay with cousins in Australia, as our education was not going well in Malaya. It was 1941, and in those days of piston-engine aircraft it took us three days to fly from Singapore to Adelaide. There were stops in Indonesia and then Darwin, where we overslept and nearly missed the connection because no one thought to wake us. My father was not best pleased when he discovered that the Prince and Princess of Siam (now Thailand) had been boarded at the last minute, which meant that I had to sit on Rosamond's knee throughout the long flight; nor, as she told me recently, was my sister.

Later, my mother came to Australia, intending to return with us to Malaya. While she was there, however, the Japanese invaded Malaya. To everyone's surprise the invasion had started in the far north of the country, avoiding the guns of Singapore pointing south out to sea. In their lightning sweep down the Malay Peninsular the Japanese had chanced upon my father who had returned, loyally, from Kuantan to pay his workers. He and the Forestry Commission officer were sitting outside the small factory when the Japanese encountered them, and having no use for prisoners the invaders marched the men into the trees, shot them, and moved on.

My father was believed dead and the Japanese were in control of Malaya but my mother, sister and I had already moved from Adelaide to Perth. We had crossed the country by train and I remember buying boomerangs from a group of Aborigines along the way, although I never learned to throw them properly. In Perth, a family took pity on us and invited us to stay at their farm up country. There I shared a room with the four sons of the house and they, tough nuts all, taught me how to aim and fire a rifle, and also how not to aim, as I tried at first with the gun on my nose.

My mother was desperate to get us all back to England, yet with little money and very few other resources it seemed we might be stranded in Australia. In the end we returned to Adelaide in 1942, boarded a cargo vessel, and sailed via the Panama Canal and so up to

New York where we joined a convoy to cross the Atlantic. During the passage two of the convoy's ships were sunk by U-boats. This must have put the remaining ships' passengers on edge but, oblivious to the fears of others, myself and another boy used to march around the decks imitating the wail that the siren sounded to warn of attack. I also recall eating as much butter as possible; we knew that there was rationing in Britain long before we made landfall in Bristol in early 1943.

Back in England we stayed with aunts (my mother's sisters). Money remained very tight until my mother was able to sell an orchard, which my father had bought in Essex before the war, and buy a small house in Chislehurst, south of London. There, when the doodlebugs (V1 rockets) came over, we used to shelter in the cupboard under the stairs. We would hear their engine noise, then came that ominous silence, and then the explosion. I am not sure whether the later V2 rockets were better or worse: there was no engine noise so you only knew one had arrived when you heard the detonation.

Prep school and beyond

I was sent as a boarder to Carn Brae, a prep school in Bromley where every morning we formed a queue, stated whether or not our bowels had opened, and were then given a spoonful of malt. After Carn Brae, aged thirteen, I went to Bradfield College near Reading; I had won a classics exhibition and this helped a little towards the fees. Bradfield was typical of most public schools of the era. Fagging and caning, which we considered perfectly acceptable but both of which are generally frowned upon today, were part of school life. The headmaster had been highly decorated in the First World War and partly because of that an unspoken, subconscious ethos of toughness and challenge underpinned life at Bradfield.

The day started with a cold shower (when I was a prefect I would try and stay in longer than anyone else as an example), and there was cross-country running and boxing, for which I was in the team. I became deputy head boy and captain of football. I loved it all.

After school came National Service in the Royal Marines from 1953–1955. The commando course took place on bleak Dartmoor and then it was out to Egypt, guarding the Canal zone. Next we were off to Malta on a destroyer with our commanding officer, Colonel Tailyour, who later became Commandant General, Royal Marines. He had us raid a deserted North African fishing village, manned for the exercise by a Guards battalion. The Navy landed us short of the beach, as usual, so we had to wade ashore, carrying our rifles high. A machine gun opened up, but in a raid speed is of the essence so we ignored it and ran swiftly on into the village. We crossed a beach 'under fire', moved quickly down the mole and 'blew up' the lighthouse at the far end. On the way back we ignored a signpost which looked as if it had been turned around, an old trick, and met up with the returning landing craft.

Towards the end of my time in Malta we were offered the choice between taking a parachute course or a cliff leader's course when we returned to the UK. I chose rock climbing and was trained in Cornwall and North Wales by the Royal Marines, first in Tricouni nailed boots to learn good climbing technique, and then in boots with grippy, Vibram rubber soles. No protecting running belays, just long run-outs of the climbing rope: those were the days, and I have never looked back. Climbing had become my hobby and a challenge, for life.

In the 1950s, officers in the Royal Marines (it was different in the army) could only sign on for either two or twenty-two years. During my schooldays at Bradfield I had become a committed Christian, and the feeling that I was probably 'meant' to be ordained was the main reason behind me not signing on for life in the Royal Marines.

After National Service I went to Cambridge. I read history and then archaeology and anthropology, I played football for Jesus College and was an active member of the college and university Christian Unions. Immediately before I began my final year I became certain of my vocation: I received what I felt was a definite call to be ordained as a 'pastor and teacher' within the Church of England when a passage I was reading in the Letter to the Ephesians lit up for me personally, and a book I was reading confirmed, personally, the Church of England aspect. I have always been grateful for these definite callings, as in another sense I was not a 'natural'.

Ordination and chaplaincy

For various reasons my ordination training was deferred, so I worked for a year in London at the Mayflower Family Centre in Canning Town: rough, docklands territory with its fair share of gangland shootouts. David Sheppard, the England batsman who later became Bishop of Liverpool, was the warden and a commanding figure of whom I was a little in awe. My role, under an incredible character named George Burton, focused largely on the teenagers' youth club. Burton had been brought up in Glasgow's Gorbals area and, prior to his dramatic conversion to Christ, he had served in the Palestine Police, ideal experience for heading up the youth work in the East End.

Three years at Oak Hill Theological College led to my ordination in Salisbury Cathedral followed by a brief spell as a curate at St John's Church in Weymouth, in Dorset. As well as my church duties, I discovered here the unclimbed limestone cliffs of Lulworth and Portland. As this is a book about adventure, suffice to say that for the next 10 years or so I enjoyed almost exclusive development of those cliffs and eventually wrote up the Lulworth and Portland sections for the Climbers' Club *Dorset* climbing guide of 1977.

After what may have been the church's shortest ever curacy, a mere eighteen months, Mike Whinney, the warden of the Cambridge University Mission in Bermondsey, needed an ordained Boys' Club Leader and I returned to youth work in London, spending three happy years at the CUM as it was called, in Bermondsey. It was hard work but I loved it, challenging as it was in its own right, and it became obvious to me that this downtown youth work was really more my vocation. And here I met and married Kate, who was a ward sister on the male surgical ward at University College Hospital. We met in a field at Woolacombe, North Devon – in those days youth clubs used to run large tented camps under canvas by the seaside for the boys and girls of the club. In spite of running my car into the back of her beloved VW Beetle, we were married in Bermondsey, and then together we crossed the Thames to North London and the Oxford Kilburn Club, where I took over as warden.

In Cockney Bermondsey there had been a strong community spirit: not so in Kilburn, where the original terraced houses were being demolished and replaced by high-rise flats. It proved another challenging three years, featuring a drunken right-hander that knocked back my front teeth after I asked a man not to pee against our club's front door. On the bright side, at CUM we would take groups of boys on climbing weekends in North Wales, and at Kilburn I took groups climbing and camping to Portland. Such trips were occasional but I am encouraged to have heard since that some of the boys recall them as high points in their lives.

Then came an offer I could not refuse: chaplain and outdoor pursuits master at St David's College in Llandudno. The school took boys who were dyslexic or otherwise struggling with conventional education and focused on sport, the arts and practical subjects in addition to the academic side. I was employed to take the boys mountain walking, climbing and skiing, and the Sunday services were my domain, as was teaching religious education. As a teacher I did not excel; I had more success building Royal Marines-type assault courses in the school grounds. We also made several new rock climbing routes on the Great Ormes' Hornby Crags, one of which ended up with me shooting down the cliff. All three protecting runners pulled out and I was only stopped a foot or two before hitting the ground when the rope became tangled around the second's body. He had, until then, been snoozing quietly on the belay ledge. It did not prevent us from going back another day to complete the climb, but I have never ceased to remind my second, Denis, of the incident ever since as a joke between us.

So we made a number of new routes here and on other cliffs on the Ormes. I suppose part of the motivation was that the lads now found something they could do well and gained confidence. Another challenge we undertook for instance was at the end of summer terms when the exams were over and done with, after bivying for the night at the top of Snowdon, or at the other end of the Carneddau depending on which way round we were doing it, we would traverse the sixteen 3000-foot peaks of Snowdonia in a day; it was exacting but a wonderful experience, and I have lost count of the number of times we did it.

I also trained boys here for the Duke of Edinburgh's Award. One boy, Richard Wallis, achieved his Gold Award. This had taken quite a bit of organising, especially the final expedition, as I had to organise relays of boys in school time to accompany him day and night over the four days (he was not allowed to walk the mountains or camp on his own for safety reasons). When we went to Buckingham Palace for Richard to receive his Gold Award, I was put in charge of one of the groups. The Duke of Edinburgh came round to see the candidates and give the Awards, and stopped 'Why are you here?' he asked. 'Well, I am a climber, Your Royal Highness', I replied. 'Yes but why are *you* here'. I had forgotten I was wearing my clerical collar. He moved swiftly on. So typical of me to talk at cross purposes with the Duke of Edinburgh, the only time I was ever likely to go to the Palace.

After eight years at St David's we made a family move to Scotland where I worked as chief instructor at the Carnoch Outdoor Centre in Glencoe. Many of the centre's activities were taught at a fairly basic level, but from time to time throughout the year we ran more advanced courses in rock, snow and ice climbing, plus mountaineering, canoeing, skiing and sailing. I held a Mountaineering Instructor Certificate from my time at St David's, but now managed to add to that a British Canoe Union Senior Instructor (Sea) and a British Association of Snowsport Instructors Level 2, as it is termed now.

Around that time Kate and I bought *Faraway*, a former Admiralty pilot cutter converted to a gaff-rigged ketch. It was a choice between this old wooden boat full of character and a slightly more expensive, reasonably modern Albin Vega glassfibre boat. My wife went for the character. So, by now in our forties, and learning mainly from books, we began to sail on the west coast of Scotland. The family expedition we made to Northern Ireland was a big undertaking for us in those days. There were seven of us and two of the children had to sleep under the cockpit cover when we were at anchor.

After three years or so in Scotland, in 1980 I was appointed chaplain at Kingham Hill School on the Oxford-Gloucester border. A Christian foundation, the school had been set up by Charles Baring Young towards the end of the nineteenth century for 'those in boarding need' and many of its pupils came from broken homes. Pupils such as these were obviously ripe for outdoor pursuits, so as well as running the chapel services and teaching religious education, I made skiing, windsurfing and sailing part of the activities. I also organised a few parachute jumps and have to say that parachuting is one of the most frightening things I have ever tried. Again, I built Marines-type assault courses (Health and Safety would have gone mad), and I joined the Combined Cadet Force, founding and running a commando section, which I am pleased to say often won the inter-schools competitions at Longmoor.

By the time I got there the school was just beginning to charge fees for those who could afford it, but there was a huge bursary fund for those who could not. The Kingham Hill Trust had just liquidated £1.5 million to refurbish the school, while still attempting to maintain the same sort of emphasis, 'for those in boarding need'. Some pupils were referred by local authorities, although some of these were a bit too hot to handle and did not last the pace in a boarding school environment. They could be anything from sons of Service families to those with dyslexia, with a strong emphasis on broken homes and single parent families.

Coming from some years working with youth in tough areas such as the East End and Kilburn (even worse), I identified easily with these boys and especially the 'baddies'. To be honest they seemed to love 'the Rev', perhaps because of the activities I was bringing them, and I got on famously with them, never calling them by their proper names (an East End habit), which they seemed to enjoy. They also enjoyed my Wednesday 'stories to make a point' in chapel, although you had to be quick with the point after the story before the feet began to shuffle. One Sunday service I climbed up into the rafters past the small statue of the founder and fell off onto the rope as an example of faith. Of course both schools were boys only; I would have been hopeless with girls, having no real experience of working with them in the past, and feeling that not many would have enjoyed my rather tough, hearty approach (but I could be wrong!).

When we sold our house in Scotland we bought a 'proper' boat, a 33-foot Westerly Discus, but a combination of the children finding other things to do and Kate's seasickness meant that I began to use the boat more and more for the school. I took the boys sailing, first to the Channel Isles and France and then to the Azores. In 1986, two years after the Azores, we marked the school's centenary with our 'First School Across the Atlantic and Back' voyage. We set off on a major expedition every two years – some are recounted later in the book – and in the intervening years we made our Channel Isles' trips.

Retirement into action

After twelve years at Kingham I was asked to leave. Maybe I was a little too independent. Or perhaps my teaching had let me down: I had, under the eyes of a school inspector who had sat in on a class one morning, given a pretty disastrous lesson to a class of the younger boys (the younger lads were never my strong suit in any case).

In 1992, having been jettisoned into early retirement, we decided to head back up to Scotland. Kate, who had been the district nurse for the West Highland region in the late 1970s (and being Irish was Celtic anyway so had instant rapport), was very keen to return. We had already bought a small stone cottage up there – small was all we could afford, having bought the boat – and I continued planning the 'First School Group to Sail Round the World' voyage with some of Kingham's school leavers. The chairman of governors was dead set against the school being involved but I was, finally, allowed to use Kingham Hill's name. Fortunately the trip was a huge success, with two of the lads staying on the whole way round and changing two at six or seven places round the world.

Our circumnavigation included Antarctica, but it had taken three months to get there and it would take another three to get back. However, you could sail to the Arctic and back in the same summer, and so after the circumnavigation I began my Tilman-type expeditions to Greenland and Arctic Canada: combining sailing with climbing from the boat.

To earn money towards the boat's upkeep I had been ski instructing during the winters in France. Early one season there was an urgent phone call from my daughter-in-law; Anna, our adopted daughter, was in intensive care at John Radcliffe Hospital in Oxford. During the Vietnam War, Kate and I had adopted Peter and Anna, two mixed race American-Vietnamese children from Danang orphanage where, it was rumoured, there were sometimes five to a cot. We already had two children of our own and their new brother and sister fitted in seamlessly; then two years later Rachel was born.

Just before Christmas Anna had caught a severe dose of flu and, complicated by recurring lupus, which is very difficult to treat, she became unconscious. Her condition worsened and, ultimately, Kate had to make the decision to allow her life support machines to be turned off. Agonising as it was, as a former nurse Kate was better equipped than the rest of the family to make such a decision. Anna was buried in the town cemetery. All this cost us dear; as someone said at the time, 'They were a close-knit family'.

At times like these there is never any answer to the question 'Why?' We cannot be told or expect to know everything in this life. We returned home, saddened, but determined to take up life again.

Indeed life must go on, and later that summer I embarked on a fresh expedition – I would sail to the Arctic with a party of climbers who would attempt to scale the 900-metre wall of *Sandersons Hope*.

This sparked a pattern of Arctic summer expeditions and, to fund the boat, winter ski instructing. Then in 2002 a new means of earning a crust presented itself: I was offered the job of paid skipper delivering a friend's boat from Cape Canaveral to Scotland (*see* 'Mutiny' on the *Palandra*, page 122).

When two years later, wintering alone in Arctic Greenland, I lost the first *Dodo's Delight* to fire (*see* Prologue, page xv), my son David said, 'You'll just have to come back and start again', and of course he was right. The insurers, Yachtsure, played absolutely straight and paid out for total loss. I was therefore able to look for a replacement boat and, having considered one or two other options, decided to replace like with like, tracking down another Discus near Plymouth. As the original *Dodo* was now under the water in Greenland, the Register of British Shipping allowed me to transfer her name: *Dodo's Delight* lived again.

It took around three years to bring the Discus up to the standard I wanted. She had some osmosis* but two layers of tough, epoxy resin added as a replacement would, I hoped, strengthen the hull, and my son David – a boatbuilder until he took up making musical instruments – built a solid cuddy (deck shelter). All this time I was unable to sail my own boat, but I had opportunities to help others sail theirs, and to earn some cash towards the refit by taking part in adventures recounted later, which at least compensated. We would soon be ready to go.

While the boat was being fettled I had been in Bavaria, Germany, teaching downhill skiing, ski touring and mountaineering to groups of British soldiers. During a downhill session on the Fellhorn, the group had gone ahead and I tried something on my own which led

---

* A creeping affliction caused by water entering the hull skin.

to a fall. I got up, but it felt as if something was stuck in my throat and, back at the lodge, I told the chief instructor that I would 'just pop round to the hospital'. In the hospital waiting room I began to feel a lot worse, then I stopped breathing, lost consciousness and fell to the floor.

I gather the doctors were with me in a flash. They cut a slit in my throat and inserted a tube into my windpipe so that air could reach my lungs, then flew me in a helicopter – still unconscious – to Kempten hospital's intensive care unit. The diagnosis was thyroid haematoma, an internal bleed into my chest, although the cause of the bleed remains a mystery. When I first regained consciousness the hole in my throat meant I could not speak. I signalled frantically for pen and paper, but then found I could hardly write. When the hole in my throat was finally patched up, I had to put a little ball in my mouth to help me learn to talk again. Vivid, presumably drug-induced dreams form my memory of the whole episode; dreams so vivid that for a long time I could not distinguish between reality and fantasy. Even now there are some memories I cannot be sure of.

Three weeks later I was deemed just fit enough to fly home, accompanied by Kate who had flown out on news of my collapse. Luckily, all medical bills and the flight were covered by insurance and I saw the whole thing as a merciful deliverance – not keeling over until I got to hospital, for example. Once we were home I recovered reasonably quickly and was fit enough to return to ski instructing the next winter. But not with the army – I don't know why but they wouldn't have me back!

As always, I needed money to maintain the boat so off I went to Verbier, Switzerland. It was an enjoyable season's instructing, but accommodation was expensive so I ended up staying in a concrete nuclear bunker under some shops. It was not too bad except that the air had to be renewed each day, so no cooking or alcohol was allowed, and apart from occasional visits to a nearby café for pizza, dinner was always cold corned beef sandwiches. My frugality paid off and

I flew home with the 3,000 Swiss francs I had saved stuffed into my underpants to avoid the excessive Swiss bank charges.

At last, with *Dodo's Delight* ready for serious sailing we were ready for a work-up passage, and what better way to test the boat than a trip down to the Azores. I had renewed a lot of the rigging and the boom, led the controls back to the cockpit, tackled all the usual thousand and one other jobs, and in Verbier I had recruited three fellow ski instructors, all keen for the trip (*see* Azores – last visit, page 30).

So, for the last thirty years or so I have used *Dodo's Delight* for sailing and climbing expeditions. I've also managed to include some paid work skippering delivery trips, some of which have gone better than others. Latterly, I have been drawn back to the Arctic, sailing, climbing and skiing. As I write, the boat is in Alaska, where she overwintered after traversing the Northwest Passage, ready for the return, west to east. The Corps motto of the Royal Marines is *per mare, per terram*: I relished my National Service experience in the Royal Marines and my life has been, and still is, an evolving series of adventures, by sea and by land. At the age of 79 it is good still to be young...

Postscript

You've got to hand it to Ignatius Loyola (founder of the Jesuits), whether you are Catholic or not (and I am not):

> *Teach us, good Lord, to serve thee as thou deservest:*
> *to give and not to count the cost;*
> *to fight and not to heed the wounds;*
> *to toil and not to seek for rest;*
> *to labour and not to ask for any reward,*
> *save that of knowing we do thy will.*

Difficult, but would that there was more of that spirit today.

CHALLENGE IS THE NAME OF THE GAME

Well, dear, it's true that adventures are good for people even when they are very young. Adventures can get into a person's blood even if he doesn't remember having them.

THE SECRET OF PLATFORM 13, EVA IBBOTSON

Climbing

I thought I had arrived at the end of the world. I had been ordained in Salisbury Cathedral to serve as a curate in St John's Church, Weymouth. Not so long before, I had been a resident helper at the Mayflower Family Centre in the East End of London down by the old Surrey docks, long before Canary Wharf was even thought of. Now I was back at an old fashioned parish, almost Victorian in outlook in some respects, at least in those days. And what was more, this was the south coast of England, not a mountain or cliff that I thought climbable to be seen. How could a man survive?

But then, reading a climbing magazine, I saw that Joe Brown, the climbing guru of the age, had made some new climbs on limestone in Yorkshire. 'So climbing on limestone is possible and not necessarily too loose,' I thought. Followed quickly by, 'Hey, we have plenty of *limestone* cliffs round here.'

As part of my National Service in the Royal Marines I had been well trained in climbing, with commando raids in mind. In those days you started by climbing for six weeks in nailed boots, because it was 'better for your technique'. And there was no such thing as protection, rather the maxim that 'a leader must not fall'. You did not question authority in those days – if you were told to 'climb in nailed boots and run the rope out', you climbed in nail boots and ran the rope out.

So I started to climb on and develop the cliffs of Lulworth and Portland (which virtually nobody had done before), mainly with my church youth group. Legends abounded, such as I was wearing my climbing gear beneath my clergy robes. You must believe what you will!

We started with Lulworth, driving over in the evenings in my old blue A40 car, parking near the cliffs and rushing round to the bottom to start the climbs from sea level. Later we moved to Portland where it looked as if the shorter but extensive cliffs on the east side might give some good routes on good rock, which they did. I got my wrist slapped slightly for not including any religious content in these 'church' meetings, which was a fair point. With hindsight I might well have included a short Bible reading on the cliffs overlooking the sea in the evening sun, having concluded some worthy routes, which would have been wholly appropriate. But I was young, fanatical about the climbing and we often did not finish till it was getting dark.

It was a long time before I plucked up the courage to start on the west cliffs of Portland. They were bigger, more formidable and looked looser – until we tried them. We were by now wearing EBs – the forerunner of the sticky rock shoes of today – and had the beginnings of protection with chocks on wires, which you could slot into cracks as you went up, threading the climbing rope through an attached karabiner so you did not drop all the way down if you fell off. But this was long before the fantastic sure-to-hold-you cams of today which have so revolutionised climbing and its standards. We started on some low-lying stuff on Fallen Slab and Battleship Buttress (most of the names I gave to features on the east and west sides are still in use today, which is rather nice) before moving on to the more formidable looking cliffs and walls themselves.

One summer day my climbing partner, Murray, and I decided to tackle a new cliff, a section called Wallsend, possibly named by the original quarrymen. There was a certain amount of secret rivalry between us as Murray was also now putting up new routes in the area, but it never came to the surface.

To start the climb we had to make our way down a grassy bank, and walk and scramble along the platforms and boulders at sea level for quite some distance north. We changed into our EBs and I put on my Whillans harness (the climbing harness of the period) and racked up our chocks and gear onto the harness, before tying onto the rope. Surveying the cliff wall, this first part didn't look too bad. It seemed best to start on the right-hand side of the face, up a crack system, and then ascend leftwards and upwards across the curious wall. Curious in that it was made up of stratas of Portland stone, with darker rock between, pock marked by centuries of wind and spray. If memory serves, it was another lovely sunny evening. I started up the vertical cracks over a small overhang which gave no trouble and placed a chock at the top of the cracks before traversing left. This was sensible technique: it is always better for the second climber if there is something above him on which the leader might be held and, anyhow, as I was about to traverse a fair way left there had to be something to keep the rope coming down vertically to him as he climbed the initial cracks.

As I had predicted, this first wall wasn't difficult. In fact it was fun because of its unusual nature, and you could look around and appreciate the scenery. I could appreciate it even more when I reached the stance higher up, on a ledge where I belayed (tied) myself onto the piton (metal spike) which I had banged into a crack in the rock on a previous attempt. This acted as an anchor for making both myself and my second safe, and I called down to Murray who began his steady climb before also tying himself into the belay.

Now the difficulties were really going to start. This was more like it, I had failed on a couple of previous attempts – was I going to make it this time? Uncertainty, challenge, risk, courage – it was all here. It was necessary to move left into another small corner and then climb steeply using cracks and small holds to gain height to reach a position where it would be possible to move further left around the jutting corner, which was probably going to constitute the main difficulty of the climb. A short, silent prayer, and I moved up slowly and carefully, placing another chock for protection before making a delicate traverse left to reach the corner. This was a bit tricky ... softly, softly now... it was pushing me out, but I reached round the corner...

made it so far... and now some delicate steps left finally got me onto an accommodating ledge where I could stand and relax, looking up at the 3-metre wall above me.

This wall had defeated me before, or rather my inability to find any holds in the steep grass over the top with which to lever myself had. There was not enough rock showing over the top to use for a mantelshelf move (pushing oneself up with hands flat on the top) and anyhow the steep grass could push you off. I was not averse to using an earth axe at the top, slamming it into the grass to use as a hand hold (a technique learnt in the Royal Marines). But when I took one up this time, I still failed to find sufficient purchase to get out at the top and had to climb back down to the ledge again. 'Is this going to go? Not another failure, please.' Only on the second attempt did I at last find some means of levering myself up onto the grass, and then found some rock for a belay higher up. Thank you, Lord!

I called down to Murray and he came up quite fast. Of course, it is always easier seconding! But he did concede that the corner was quite difficult. I probably gave him a tight rope for the top, and he was probably rude about such a finish. But we had made a new route on a totally unclimbed cliff. What elation! We called it Wallsend Wall and gave it a modest grade. I see that nowadays they have raised it into the Extreme grades and I cannot help feeling secretly pleased about that, too. (Another upgraded route, and in another story, I named *Fond Farewell* after a table-sized overhanging block I was pulling up on exploded out of the cliff and took me hurtling down with it until the rope stopped me. An ankle injury did not stop me completing the climb, so it was nearly my fond farewell.)

Among the elation is disappointment, though this relates to climbing politics. Since I stopped climbing hard, 'sport climbing' has arrived. That is to say, in certain areas bolts have been drilled into the rock and can be used to protect climbs, the idea being that you can then really push your standard to your ultimate limit, as you are sure to be held by the rope running though the carabiner or snap link suspended on the bolt if you fall off. But to me this does away with the whole essence of climbing, which is the risk to be overcome by your own skill, challenge, adventure, over and above simple technique. Where is the risk, where is the courage, if you know there is going to be no real danger? A gymnastic exercise perhaps, to improve your climbing standard, good training for the real thing. But not the real thing. To my disappointment, long after I had left the area, the whole 3 miles of this pristine hard limestone on the west side of Portland giving such superb climbing had been designated a sport climbing area. It had been agreed that the original 'trad' routes (those routes done by traditional methods, protected by your own skill as you went up and without bolts) would be left as such. I might argue that bolted climbs pander to those who lack daring and courage, and I'm relieved that most of my 'traditional' routes remain free of bolts. But imagine my bitter disappointment to see in the latest guidebook that our Wallsend Wall route, climbed by 'proper' traditional methods, had been retro-bolted. It shouldn't have been done.

Kayaking

Sometimes adventures were unintended. I had done some kayaking in the Royal Marines as training for small raids and reconnaissance, and one day early on in my explorations of Portland I decided to paddle down the west side to survey its climbing potential. I got into my old wood and canvas kayak (with no sprayhood) and launched from Chesil Beach, a difficult thing to do in itself owing to the heavy swell. Nearing Portland Bill at the end I turned the kayak nonchalantly round and started to paddle back again. I was going backwards.

I knew little about tides in those days and nothing about the ferocious tidal rips round the Bill. There was no way I could make any progress, so I had to turn and paddle round the Bill and right up the longer east coast of Portland. I stopped once and landed on a rocky shelf to consider my options, but there was no way out but to paddle on, all the way round. Even when I reached the outer breakwater enclosing Portland Harbour there were at least two more miles to paddle to reach the other side of Chesil Beach from where I had started hours previously. I arrived back in the dark, completely exhausted.

Looking back it is one of my more pleasing and abiding memories, just because I was exhausted and it had been such a challenge, on the edge of my abilities. There is almost always risk inherent in any challenge. And for risk to be real there has to be the possibility that it could all go badly wrong.

Sailing

The year was 1998 and it was our first proper climbing and sailing expedition to Greenland. When I returned from sailing round the world I asked myself 'What now?' Then I remembered how Bill Tilman, a British explorer and climber of former years, had discovered that he could sail to Greenland and back in one summer, and do some climbing over there as well. This seemed an interesting concept, as well as being convenient, and would combine both climbing and sailing. And both the sailing across the Atlantic and the climbing were going to be challenging. What more could a man want? So I started organising Tilman-type expeditions, and this was to be our first venture.

I had collected an enterprising crew. Three of them, Brian, Danoo (so called by me) and Steve, had worked that Antarctic summer for the British Antarctic Survey in various places and various capacities, so this meant they were now free for the northern summer. Then there was Annie, who liked adventure and who had sailed with me to the Faroe Islands some years before.

We set out from near my home in Appin, Scotland, on 15 June, and experienced the usual Atlantic crossing in these high latitudes. That is to say, stormy. The depressions spin up from Newfoundland across to Iceland or the Faroes and you almost always get caught by at least one gale in the middle. Fifteen days into the passage and some 140 miles south of Cape Farewell, that notorious Cape of Storms, we were running before on bare poles – we had taken all sails down and were still doing 4 to 5 knots. Brian had gone up to help Annie on the helm and at one stage I stuck my head out and asked them 'How is it going?' 'We're just in control, but only just,' said Brian. Afterwards he told me it had gusted to 61 and 65 knots of wind around this time. Danoo was on watch next and I went up to be supportive. It was wild, but we were in control, though Danoo was having some difficulty anticipating on the helm. Steve came up for the next watch and clipped on.

Annie was on cooking duty that day and, under the circumstances, wisely decided she would just cut up fruit cake and heat up custard to go with it. Danoo had got into her bunk on the far side of the aft cabin for security and I was sitting on a seat nearby. I was just saying to her 'I really think it is beginning to moderate…' when there was a loud bang and I found myself flying through the air across the cabin and landing on Danoo in her bunk. The lady was not amused: I had covered her with custard – hair, face, sleeping bag, the lot. When the boat righted itself I thought it best to beat a hasty retreat, and anyhow I was sure that bang must have meant we had lost the mast, and so rushed up into the cockpit to check. What a relief when I saw the mast was still standing.

So what had happened and what was the damage? Steve told us that a huge freak wave had suddenly come up unawares from astern, picked up the boat, which had then shot down the near vertical front of the wave, broached sideways and crashed down into the trough at the bottom going 90 degrees over onto its side. There was no way Steve could have controlled it in those circumstances and indeed he had himself been thrown half out of the cockpit, although thankfully he was clipped on. We set about looking for damage, me with a huge blob of custard above my left eye, which my crew didn't know whether to tell me about or not.

I knew there had been a point of weakness where the forward bulkhead met the hull, and sure enough when I looked over the side there was now a longer crack in the gelcoat at that point. I emptied the locker inside as best I could and was relieved to find there was no water coming in. As long as we could sail as much as possible on starboard tack to keep this side of the hull out of the water we might be all right. At the same time I noticed that the force of the crash had pushed in all the woodwork on the starboard side by 2 inches or more. It would need repair at some point no doubt but it wasn't affecting the integrity of the boat.

The wind had moderated by now and so we were able to sail on. I was relieved but at the same time wary, and kept checking the locker for water ingress. All seemed to be well. I took the boat too close to Cape Farewell and the south coast of Greenland where ice collects, and so we had to spend time weaving and dodging brash and growlers before eventually rounding Cape Desolation and making our way up to Nuuk.

With accidents like this, as with falling off rock climbs, it all happens so quickly you don't have time to be frightened. Afterwards can be the trying time. And now at Nuuk there was the concern of having to spend expedition time on a repair, and I wondered what it was going to cost and whether we were going to be able to continue with the expedition after all. But in the end Anders Nillson, at the time the only Danish member of the Greenland Home Rule Parliament in Nuuk, lent us his boat cradle. A crane lifted us out admittedly at some expense, and Peter the harbourmaster, at least of the local yacht club, marked out a wide area round the crack and ground it down with an angle iron until the crack disappeared, before building it up again with layer upon layer of fibreglass. There were some shenanigans as I insisted on lifting out again for another small crack to be filled, but I think the crew forgave me for the delay, especially as the expedition could now continue after all. It had been a stressful time, and yes there can be risk within challenge, there almost has to be, but maybe 'fortune favours the brave' – or foolish?

So … an adrenalin junkie?

People have asked me, why do you have this lust for adventure? The short answer is I do not really know. But if you had been to a public school where your headmaster had risen to lieutenant colonel in his twenties in the First World War, and had so many Military Crosses and Croix de Guerres for bravery and successful operations, and then you had been an officer yourself in the Royal Marines Commandos in Egypt, Malta and North Africa, and the Commando Cliff Assault Wing, how else would you be? And as I have written elsewhere I cannot begin to describe the feeling when you are treading territory where nobody else has ever before walked or been on God's good earth (and yes, my faith does have something to do with this, and the joy of God's creation), and experience the elation of making the first ascent of a hard rock climb on which you might or might not have succeeded, or even one not so hard, but which nobody has ever climbed before. And maybe there is an element of escapism here, too. If you are engaged on a hard rock climb or a challenging experience it is impossible to think of anything else and the tensions of life fall away.

When I started sailing, quite late in life having been a fanatical rock climber for twenty-five years as well as a 'priest' (or minister), I unconsciously assumed that all sailors were automatically secretly hoping to round Cape Horn. It took me quite some time before I realised that not all sailors actually *wanted* to sail round Cape Horn. But I still cannot quite understand people who are content just to 'sail for pleasure', sailing from one anchorage to another, in the Mediterranean or Caribbean for instance, eating a pleasant meal ashore in a taverna and sleeping peacefully back on the boat for the night. Very pleasant for a bit of a break from more difficult sailing, or even from the stresses of the office, but for me at least it seems there must be challenge and achievement of a goal for it to be really satisfying. And often adventure involves risk, which must then be managed, but challenge gives the ultimate satisfaction.

OK you will say, so the man is mad. But if that is so then it is a wonderful way to be. God has given me a wonderful life…

02

MIDDLE EARTH

Great oaks from little acorns grow.
14TH CENTURY PROVERB

Adventure to one man is a walk in the park to another. For us, a school chaplain and his pupils and former pupils, our nursery slopes were the Azores, to which we made some voyages in the 1980s and 90s, initially as a prelude to more ambitious trips in our newly acquired *Dodo's Delight*. Some of our mishaps seem tame now but to us at the time, new to ocean sailing, they were real challenges. Our first visit to the Azores in 1984 was also our first ocean passage. It is worth comparing that with our last visit in 2008. Much changed in the intervening years, particularly with regard to navigational devices, and even the Azores themselves were a shadow of their former selves.

AZORES OR BUST

'It's only 700 miles to Falmouth', we yelled as Dickie, one of Kingham's finest, floated away. We were on our way back from the Azores and the lads had taken to playing human Poohsticks in the Atlantic one afternoon: jumping off the bow, swimming round to the stern, catching the boarding ladder and climbing back up. It was interesting that Dickie, who seemed on a fairly even keel at school, should now be showing signs of a more adventurous spirit. He had jumped, missed the ladder and was now adrift. We left him to sweat, or swim, for a while, then turned back to pick him up.

This was my first ocean passage aboard *Dodo's Delight* with pupils from Kingham Hill School, where I was chaplain. The boat was so named by our daughter, Rachel. The nine prospective boat names we had submitted so far to the British Registry of Shipping all turned out to have been taken by other vessels and we were running short of ideas when Rachel came up with *Dodo's Delight*. It was the title of a delightful children's book she was reading, and we still have it somewhere. I had thought of calling the boat *Sea Shuttle*, but in view of what the iconic transatlantic sailor and Cockleshell war hero Blondie Hasler observed on the subject of boat names, I am glad Rachel saved the day. Hasler's advice was to go up in to the Scottish hills (he lived in Scotland), shout the boat's name and imagine what it would sound like over the VHF at two o'clock in the morning.

Inspired by the success of our English Channel cruises we were ready for an ocean; or at least part of the Atlantic, I decided. I would take a crew of four (three Kingham Hill boys and my son Petey, ranging from fifteen to eighteen years in age) from Falmouth down to the Azores. There was nothing to stop us. The year was 1984 and the Health and Safety Executive, the apparent enemy of risk and adventure, was infinitely less bothersome than it is today. The myriad of paperwork and personal checks that would be needed now for a crew of youngsters to sail an ocean in a small boat skippered by a chaplain does not bear thinking about.

The three Kingham Hill boys were the aforementioned Dickie, and Will and Bob. Will and Bob were great friends, and about to leave the school. Slightly contrasting characters, Will was perhaps the steadier of the two; Bob a little taller and more ebullient and fanciful. They both got bitten by the sailing bug and soon after leaving the school they signed on to another boat to help sail her across the Atlantic via the Canaries to the Caribbean, and later Will established a successful yacht charter business in the British Virgin Islands.

In the 1980s a passage to the Azores was still considered something of a challenge, not least because navigation was by means of the sextant; since GPS and reliable communication systems have become commonplace navigation has been easier and more certain.

In Falmouth we posted a notice on the boat: 'Azores or Bust'. At that age, theirs and mine, it was all an adventure, a challenge, and it didn't really occur to us that we might possibly fail. But any hubris there might have been was tempered with the knowledge that the Swedish skipper tied up next to us had recently returned from sailing round the world, much of it alone. He told me that an empty beer crate was the best sea anchor he had ever used, so for years I carried one at *Dodo*'s stern, although, fortunately, I never had cause to test it by throwing it over the side in a storm.

Navigating with a sextant takes practice, patience and clear-headed arithmetic (never my strong suit). I well remember the first sextant shot I took 'in anger'. Ashore on solid ground I had practised bringing the sun down to the horizon and it did not prove too difficult. At sea, off the western seaboard of Europe, it was a different matter and the position I computed put us 60 miles inland – in Spain. I re-checked the figures and re-did the maths and, to my great relief, managed to find and correct my mistake. Now we knew where we were.

My skill with the sextant improved steadily and the Azores popped up on cue. Frustratingly, for most of the voyage we had little or no wind. At last a strong westerly blew, which drove us southwards towards Santa Maria meaning we had to tack back up north overnight, passing the rocks and flashing light beacon of Isla das Formigas rather too close for comfort. The crew called me, but they were fast becoming competent to handle the situation themselves.

In the morning the headland of Ponta da Madrugada on the south-eastern tip of the island of São Miguel came into view. By then the strong winds had fallen away to virtually nothing and we spent the whole day ghosting in whatever slight breeze we could find along the southern shore to Ponta Delgada. How many boats have had to attach dinghy paddles to genoa poles to inch an 8-tonne boat across the finish line as we had to at Ponta Delgada? Our plan had always been to sail the entire voyage under racing conditions and, therefore, not use the engine at all, which proved no mean feat in the conditions we experienced. We fulfilled our aim, but it did make for a slow passage.

Somehow that first voyage to the Azores has always seemed the best. We had our little adventures, both going and returning. One night on the outward passage I was woken up by Bob, one of the crew. 'You had better come up and have a look, Rev.' There, dead ahead, was another sailing boat creeping gently towards us in the night, sails up, navigation lights on, with light somehow illuminating the boat as well. It sailed serenely on, we altered course to avoid it, it passed us by, and at no time did we see a soul aboard. Then it glided silently away. Our own *Marie Celeste*…

The return passage threw up a few memorable moments, one of which had a sting in its tail. Intrigued by the Portuguese men-of-war, the crew lifted some of the venomous creatures aboard in a bucket of water and had a closer look before chucking them back. Some hours later Bob picked up the bucket and gave a loud yelp, stung by a stray tentacle left inside. Bob felt quite ill through the night and although the rest of us didn't take him too seriously (he was perhaps a little prone to dramatics), his friend Will, a caring lad, looked after him.

Apart from the men-of-war we saw a number of turtles on both the outward and return passages, and remembering the Robertson family who had largely survived on them when shipwrecked in the Pacific in the 1970s, we tried but failed to catch one. Even if we had we would not have had the guts to kill it, nor the need to: unlike the Robertsons starving in their liferaft, we had plenty of food. Nevertheless, the thought of turtle steaks was tempting.

On our way home, off the Bay of Biscay in big winds and seas, we hove-to under a backed storm sail. A more conventional method is to make the jib and mainsail balance each other out to stop the boat and ride out a gale, but the strain on the violently fluttering mainsail worried me. Our rig had the rather unusual effect of bringing the wind over our starboard quarter, from slightly astern. The waves were huge, but we were not too uncomfortable, so we lay like this for twenty-six hours to let the depression move through. Over the years we have had to heave-to on a number of occasions, but for better or worse I have never used that particular sail plan again. On the whole it seems better to try and bring the bow slightly up into wind and waves, or even to lie broadside to the waves with all sail down.

Safely back and tied up alongside a pontoon in Falmouth, I had an interesting illustration of the power of addiction. Bob had run out of cigarettes miles back in the Atlantic and I, in my innocence, thought he would grab the chance to quit. Not a bit of it. When his relatives came down to meet him the first thing Bob did was cadge a fag, and another to put behind his ear for when he had finished the first. In addition to feeding his nicotine habit, Bob was also interviewed about our voyage by BBC Radio 1 and the crew were thrilled to hear it broadcast next day. Of course you might argue that I never gave up my addiction (to adventure) either. True, but whereas smoking is positively harmful, adventure can only be character forming and help to equip you in attitude for the challenges of life! Well, that's the theory…

The Azores

The voyage was exciting, but it was the Azores themselves that really delighted us. The islands were in those days unspoilt, or at least largely undeveloped, and there were no marinas for visiting yachts, only a small harbour for local boats. Both in Ponta Delgada and at Horta you simply tied up at the stone quayside at the far end of their respective harbour walls, or anchored off, as indeed was the case in all the harbours throughout the archipelago (I remember scolding the crew in Horta, as stepping carelessly off the quayside directly onto the boat they were tramping the island's black volcanic dust all over the decks). It was, even in those days, considered obligatory to paint your picture with the names of the crew and boat on the breakwater at Horta. At that time all the pictures were painted on the outer breakwater and ours there has long since faded to dust, as have all the rest.

We didn't spend much time in the Azores on that first visit, but it was still long enough for Dickie to go flying in the air suspended on a spinnaker off the bow of a French boat as it sailed the length of Horta harbour. A forerunner perhaps of parascending, this spinnaker flying, if you avoided being impaled on the bow when you finally let go, and it was at the very least good practice for human Poohsticks later on.

In-betweens

On subsequent visits we explored the Azores more fully and had several of the kind of adventures that in the light of what was to come might seem rather tame. One year, for example, it was a struggle just getting there, and something of a shock for my inexperienced crew. The cables on our wheel steering had broken some 300 miles from the islands. Westerlys are well built, strong boats, but their emergency steering system, at least on their Discus class, comprised a massive upright iron bar with big arms either side, which slotted directly on to the top of the rudder stock. It took a tremendous effort to crank the rudder. No doubt it was good for our upper body strength, and eventually with much heaving and pushing we did make it to Horta without mishap. But we were all younger in those days.

Another year the crew went across the strait from Horta to Madelena and climbed the well-defined triangular peak of Pico. There was no technical difficulty involved, but at over 9000 feet it is a long climb and in the Azores the heat can be a problem, and so it was. They returned in the evening elated, but very weary and weak from the heat.

Yet another year we descended into the depths of the sulphurous caldera of Graciosa. Having looked around the huge grotto for a while, we climbed into the boat provided and rowed out to the middle of the dark, spooky, steaming lake of Orpheus to admire the weird and wonderful colours and rock formations within the caldera. Unfortunately it also turned out to be the very best way of getting a splitting, day-long headache. Then, back at the harbour, we had to row ourselves and our gear to the boat in relays because the outboard motor would not start; a local fisherman finally solved the problem by changing the spark plug. You can feel very stupid sometimes.

There was also the occasion when we nearly hit the new breakwater, then still under construction, at Velas on São Jorge. This time it was *Dodo*'s engine which would not start. We had to winch up the anchor, rapidly raise sail, turn and sail out of the harbour. We rounded up just in time to miss the breakwater and made it out to sea, but it was a close run thing.

Close shaves, both minor and more serious, continued. One year we tried out our newly acquired diving skills in a bay round the corner, to the south of Horta. We were taken by motorboat to the bay where, in an underwater caldera, we dived among fantastic rock formations including a strange, cave-like cleft. I had finned out to look at the huge, sheer, vertical drop-off to the depths below but, enthralled, lost track of time; I started to run out of air and quickly surfaced. The sea was choppy and, gasping for breath, I kept swallowing water. Steve, alias Dood (who by now had been on several expeditions with me and had become an experienced sailor), swam to the rescue, towing me in the water back to the motorboat. He was rather annoyed – understandably so, as it was not the first time I had run out of air diving. But in his kindly way he never took it up with me afterwards.

So over the years the trips to the Azores, our nursery slopes of adventure, have given us much entertainment and some moments of drama, perhaps as a precursor, a testing ground to more serious ventures in later years.

AZORES – LAST VISIT

At Flores in the Azores Sir Richard Grenville lay,
And a pinnace like a fluttered bird came flying from far away.
THE REVENGE, ALFRED, LORD TENNYSON

It is worth recounting our last passage to the Azores, by way of comparison. Much had changed over the two decades. Nearly all boats now have GPS of course, which enables, or perhaps we might say entices, many people to cross oceans who probably would not and maybe should not have done so before, and (dare one say it) perhaps should not even now, without having gained an 'apprenticeship of experience'. My crews had changed (they were now adults) and so had the Azores themselves. Every harbour now has a marina, with showers, washing machines and even Wi-Fi. The remoteness, the self-sufficiency and seamanship are lost, as is much of the challenge.

Nevertheless, the outward leg of our voyage in 2008 proved more gruelling than it had in 1984; we might even on occasion have welcomed the calms of that first expedition. For a start the distance was greater. I was now living in Scotland, the land of my forefathers (or so I believe – my middle name is McIntire). Earlier that summer, while sailing round Mull for my charity Enterprise Sailing (a charity I had formed originally to help with the round the world voyage in the 90s) with a school group from downtown Birmingham, the gearbox developed a strange symptom – it was fine in reverse but slipped badly in forward gear. We sailed the boat back to Kilmelford Yacht Haven where the boatyard removed the gearbox and sent it to Manchester for repair. After the carriers had caused long delays it finally came back and was refitted.

By this time my crew for the Azores had already arrived: Rob, his wife Ali, and Mark, all ski instructors whom I had met in Verbier. They weren't experienced sailors but were up for the challenge of an ocean passage, and wanted to learn. They had already been waiting around for a week, so after a brief engine test we put out from Kilmelford for the Azores. But when we put the engine in gear and opened up the throttle we realised that the gearbox was not much better than it had been before.

We dropped anchor under sail close to shore and after a night's sleep, plus consulting together the next morning, decided to sail for the Azores anyway: we had run out of time to take the gearbox out again, send it away, have it repaired and then refitted. The boatyard at Kilmelford agreed with our decision, although I am not sure they fully realised how far we intended to go.

A favourable breeze let us sail safely through Cuan Sound in spite of its rocks and fast tidal streams then, after a frustrating day of calms, the wind set in strongly from the north and bowled us along at a great pace. We tried to put in to Scalasaig on Colonsay to top up with fresh water, but the swell was far too great for us to moor alongside the pier, and we only just managed to squeeze back out against the onshore wind, motor sailing but with precious little help from the engine.

The north wind obligingly persisted and we broad reached and ran south past Malin Head and down the west coast of Ireland. The strong northerly from astern was ideal for speed and direction, but when sailing downwind most boats do roll. The three crew were all fit from skiing in Verbier, but they had done little sailing and suffered badly from seasickness for the first three days. I did begin to wonder if it had been such a good idea to take comparative beginners on an ocean passage. On the upside, it made the catering easy for the first few days, and all strength to them: they stood their watches, however bad they were feeling. It helped that we had got the windvane self-steering working, although using it downwind did accentuate the boat's yawing. On the fourth day the wind moderated, the crew began to recover and they were fine for the rest of the voyage.

This Azores trip was intended by way of a work-up passage for crew and boat: the crew because they were planning to sail to Greenland with me the following year, and the boat because it was the replacement for my original *Dodo's Delight* and I needed to test her out on a less exacting ocean passage first. Fortunately for both these aims the wind continued steadily from the north and we soon sped away from the south-west corner of Ireland into deeper water and proper Atlantic rollers.

The boat's original sprayhood had disintegrated beyond repair and before setting out from Kilmelford we had fixed an old sail over the tubular stainless steel framework above the main hatch to make a makeshift new one. Our new hood had no windows and therefore no forward visibility, so while the crew were chatting one morning out on the bridge deck under shelter, they failed to notice a yacht crossing close-to across our bows. Not, that is, until it appeared round the far side of the boat and hood. It gave them quite a shock. However, it was daylight and the crew in the other yacht's cockpit must have seen us and taken avoiding action. Careless perhaps, but my crew of ski instructors were on a steep learning curve.

To my surprise the wind stayed in the north and continued steady, even after we were well into the Azores High. By now we were enjoying the occasional sunny day, balmier temperatures and warmer water. Ski instructors like to keep active and there is not a lot of opportunity for that within the confines of a small boat. So, led by Ali, they took to climbing somewhat gingerly down the aft boarding ladder to be trailed along behind the boat, tied on with a complicated system of ropes and knots. With fresh water at a premium on longer passages on small boats, this activity also afforded some sort of a bath, albeit in salt water. Again, it was not quite the human Poohsticks so enjoyed by the 1984 crew, but maybe this time we were going a little too fast for that.

It was around this time that Ali felt compelled to explain how being left handed hampered her ability to steer the boat. Being left handed, she told us, meant that her brain was the 'other way around' which in turn meant that she could not really tell left from right, which made it difficult for her to know which way to turn the wheel when steering. As a skier she knew to press down her right foot to turn left on the snow and I wondered if she might have found it less confusing to steer with a tiller.

At the same time as enjoying good banter together we were making rapid progress southwards, and after some fourteen days one evening we caught our first glimpse of lights from the land looming through the mist and darkness. The GPS position confirmed that we must be picking up the northern shore of Terceira, one of the islands of the Arquipelago dos Açores. We tacked westwards to run roughly parallel with the shore, before turning southwards again to avoid the island of Graciosa. In the morning the north shore of São Jorge was in sight, but it was here that we finally ran out of wind.

At this point we really could have done with a reliable engine. I did not want to risk causing more damage by trying to run our sick one slowly in gear; we had a considerable distance still to go to Horta. So we spent the whole day jilling about using what gentle breezes came our way, and it was not until the early hours of the next morning that we were able to round the western end of São Jorge. As we approached well off the point as I thought, I was startled to see what appeared to be rocks dead ahead. But then there was a huge flapping of wings and a great cloud of sea birds rose into the air.

We inched very slowly towards Horta. I do not remember ever before rejoicing at attaining the incredible speed of one knot. It was a beautiful sunny morning and we sat in the sun trying to catch what zephyrs of breeze we could. Finally I could stand it no longer and fired up the engine. 'I was just thinking the same,' said Rob. We found that the gear engaged better at very low revs, so we could make slow progress under engine after all. Ironically the wind piped up a little more as we approached the blunt headland just to the north of the harbour entrance, but we stayed on slow ahead through the rather disturbed tidal waters and gently entered the harbour. It had been a good work up passage: 1712 miles in sixteen days, which was not too bad for a 33-foot boat without an engine.

Horta

We did not stay long in the Azores in 1984, and it was the same this time around. But how things had changed. There were boats everywhere. In Horta, for example, where previously we had found only four visiting yachts tied up alongside the quay at the far end of the harbour, there was now a vast marina, which in recent years has expanded to take in the whole of the harbour's northern and western sides. And another terrible thing: every harbour in the Azores now has a marina. The islands are, in my view, ruined forever!

One welcome discovery I made, which only went to show my total ignorance of marinas, was that if your boat happens to have the requisite equipment (and thanks to its previous owners mine did) you can plug in to an electrical supply on the pontoon which then runs your lighting and even charges up your batteries. Most yachtsmen these days take it for granted and would laugh at my simplicity. Mains supply on a yacht? Whatever was the world coming to? For me, more used to spartan ways, it was remarkable.

One institution of long standing had not changed: Peter's Café, the yachtsman's haven in Horta, seemed just the same, except that old Peter had died and it was now run by his son José, with his grandson fast coming up behind. When I went there wearing my Peter's Café sweatshirt with its 1980s logo I was made especially welcome.

One of my motives for making this passage had been to renew the picture of *Dodo* that we had painted on another wall space in the early 1990s. I was heartened to find that, although grubby, the picture was still there, probably because it was in a rather awkward place to get at, accessible only by dinghy. As luck would have it Ali turned out to be quite an artist and, helped by Rob and Mark, she set about reviving the original picture complete with all the crew names and dates from previous visits, on what was fast becoming a large mural. To bring it up to date they added their names and the logo of the ski school we had all worked for in Verbier, European Snowsport. By the end I was feeling guilty: with its sparkling white background, smart black lettering and the striking colour picture of the *Dodo* (copied originally from its namesake children's book), and having stolen a little extra wall space from the adjacent ancient picture, our work of art looked rather overpowering. To any who may be visiting, please accept my apologies.

Of course we met a lot of kind and interesting people, as one does when sailing. A couple, David and Sue Wilson, entertained us royally aboard their smart Victoria 38 *Suerte*. And we ran into Christopher Hamblin on *Arabel*. I first met Christopher washing his clothes in a bucket on the pontoon to save the cost of the marina washing machines; a man after my own heart. Now he was making ready to set sail back to the UK singlehanded in true Joshua Slocum* style. Christopher had no windvane self-steering. Instead he talked of attaching headsail sheets to his tiller through blocks on the cockpit coaming. I gathered later that he did also have an old, unreliable electronic self-steering arm on board which I suppose might have helped, but it was quite an achievement all the same.

It was time to move on. We had an uneventful overnight sail in varied winds along the north coast of Pico and over to Angra do Heroísmo on Terceira. Getting out of Horta with hardly any engine power was easy; getting into Angra was difficult: the boat would barely move. Had we overcooked it leaving Horta? Painstakingly we edged into the harbour and went alongside the office to clear in. Negotiating the pontoons was a different story. We overshot our assigned berth, then trying to turn around hit another pontoon hard, stern on (reverse

---

* In 1895–1898, Joshua Slocum was the first man to sail around the world singlehanded.

gear still worked rather too well). Had we put a hole in the boat? No. Good. Then our aft gantry caught in the davits hanging off another boat's stern. Finally we came to rest, and apart from our slightly bent steelwork, which only confirmed my prejudice against davits, the boat was undamaged.

Angra do Heroísmo is an attractive city in which historic buildings straddle narrow streets. High above the marina on one side stands the city and a tall, imposing church, while the other is guarded by an impressive fort, part of which houses modern apartments. A plaque at the fort's entrance serves as a reminder that a British contingent was billeted here during the Second World War.

Our departure from the marina a few days later was only slightly less troublesome than our arrival. We reversed out from the pontoon against the wind then motored slow ahead, without mishap, to the marina office to clear out. But it was touch and go as we made our agonisingly slow progress out of the harbour through the breakwater arms. Would we make it? It was a great relief when we were back on the open sea and rewarded with sunshine and a freshening breeze. Our sails filled and we were able to relax and enjoy sailing with a fair wind, in fine weather, with a sparkling sea, for the next 100 miles or so that we were able to cover that day to reach the far-flung island of São Miguel.

We would be approaching Ponta Delgada from the west and at night, which is rather demanding: the coastline seems to go on forever and there are no very obvious landmarks or features along the shore. But we found our way and, not forgetting to keep 50–100 metres off the end of the breakwater to avoid underwater rocks and fallen masonry as noted in the pilot book, good use of the westerly breeze enabled us to turn north into the harbour. The westerly also let us sail through the marina entrance and all the way to the quayside by the marina office so there was no need to use our dodgy engine on the approach. I waited until the last minute before engaging reverse gear, hard, as the crew whipped down the mainsail and we came to a graceful halt alongside.

Ponta Delgada had been the first port of call on my original voyage to the Azores in 1984 and now on my last visit it was our final port of call, which was rather a pity as it is probably the least attractive port in the Azores. One year we hired a car and drove round the island, which was much more interesting and picturesque. By contrast the city is unimpressive and the harbour is not up to much. My opinion of the harbour was reconfirmed this time by, among others, the redoubtable offshore yachtswoman Sue Thatcher in her Victoria 38, *Tamar Swallow*. Sue and others we spoke to there reported the new marina extension to be very rolly in bad weather and complained about glitches in the shore facilities. We had a berth in the old marina, which was better.

The main reason for stopping in Ponta Delgada was to make crew changes. Rob and Ali had to leave; they were due on parade at three weddings, two in the UK and a third one in South Africa from which they were going on to train as game wardens for national parks. They had done well and we would miss them. Mark, brave man, was staying on for the return passage so I needed, ideally, two new crew.

Sometimes the hardest part of any expedition is finding your crew, and this was one of those times. Finally a friend, John, who is a forestry manager and consultant and lives not far from our home in Scotland, agreed to come out. And so did Jordan, a sixteen-year-old from Birmingham who had shown his mettle on our charity sailing courses on the west coast of Scotland. As far as I know he had never been out of Birmingham until he came north with his school to sail with us, but Jordan had since been in trouble with the police and it seemed a good idea to channel his energy into ocean sailing. Negotiations to allow him to join our crew were protracted but at the behest of his headmaster the police agreed to an extension of his bail, and so we had our second new crew member.

Jordan had to put up with being escorted all the way to Ponta Delgada, not because of anything to do with the police but because Mike Whinney (a friend and sometime Bishop of Birmingham) thought it safer as the boy had not travelled abroad before. I was however amused at having to sign for him on his arrival at the airport.

The return

We replenished our food supplies and filled the water tank. Thanks to our near-useless gearbox there was no need to top up with diesel. The wind was against us when we left the marina so Bruno, one of the harbour staff, kindly towed us to the entrance where, as soon as we caught the wind from the west, we were able to turn south-east and sail. We hoisted the main and Jordan immediately took charge. That is to say he immediately took over the helm and the sailing. That was Jordan for you… But alas he was soon feeling seasick and had to relinquish his place on the helm. We sped this time along the south coast of São Miguel in a fair breeze and took our departure from the Azores in 2008 using the same feature we had used as our landmark in 1984, the high hill of Ponta da Madrugada on São Miguel. And so after passing through some bizarre swirling tidal currents off this headland we sailed, once more, out into the Atlantic.

The return passage was testing. The wind this time proved varied and fickle. After an initial day making good northing, the wind headed us and it became a case of trying to find the most favourable tack towards our destination, making long ocean boards and checking our track constantly on the GPS. A shift in the wind gave us a more favourable slant for a while and then … we were becalmed. And our cranky gearbox left us effectively without an engine.

Mark didn't mind: he was a young and talented ski instructor rapidly rising to the top of the profession. Today was his birthday and he spent a large part of it diving into the sea, 270 miles out from the Azores. He managed to cajole a reluctant Jordan to join him, who immediately enjoyed it, and then an even more reluctant John, who at least said he did. They (or was it only Mark?) became more and more ambitious until they were diving off the spreaders halfway up the mast. The skipper resolutely resisted all blandishments to take a bath in such an unseamanlike manner. John had baked a cake and later that day we presented it to the birthday boy, with a rather feeble attempt on our part at lighted matches for candles. You have to find something to do when totally becalmed on a flat sea in the sun with no wind and no engine. Mark's birthday fell on the right day.

Next morning a slight breeze gave us some steerage way and the midday log entry read, 'Sunshine, breeze, south wind, what more could you want?' The following morning the log read, 'Wonderful sailing weather – sun, breeze, sailing off the wind. BUT Lavac squirting again.' And thereby hangs a tale…

On our way to the Azores the Lavac pump in the heads had developed a problem. I will spare you the exact details but when the handle was pumped to flush, foul water squirted from the junction between the pump handle and the main unit. I had stripped it down in situ, found a split in the rubber diaphragm, which I had replaced and sealed to within an inch of its life, and to our relief the leak was no more. Or so I had hoped. Now the Lavac was squirting again. Nasty. John selflessly volunteered to take a look at it and I suggested that rather than trying to fix it where it was he should take the whole thing off the bulkhead, which made it easier to work on. We could see no split in the rubber diaphragm this time, but to be safe John fitted another spare (I had been caught out before and had plenty aboard). With everything reconnected it was, once more, a case of problem solved. But would there be a next time? I resolved to buy a second complete new pump unit before my next voyage. That way I could fit a working spare then fix the failed pump when it best suited me. Such things as malignant loo pumps assume a vital importance on small boats.

There were calms. And there were gales: ship's log, '1200 gusting Force 8; hove-to (lying a-hull).' Prior to this John and I, mate and skipper respectively, had discussed the best course of action. We were reaching with three reefs in the mainsail.

'What do you think we should do, John?'

'I think we should press on.'

I gave it a moment's thought, 'Well, I reckon we should heave-to.'

Skippers can be a right pain. So we hove-to, or rather lay a-hull broadside to the waves with all sail down. This is a tactic I have used in the past, but this time it resulted in a very uncomfortable, jerky motion. John, who was always under pressure to return as quickly as possible to his business in Scotland, was in retrospect probably right. We could and perhaps should have pressed on.

Next morning as the glass rose swiftly the old adage, 'Quick rise after low foretells another blow' concerned me a little. But we had had enough of bouncing around lying a-hull, and so we set sail. We hove-to again later to make sure we were not going to be pushed too far to the south of Ireland – which caused some raised eyebrows among the crew who could see no good reason for this in the light airs we had at the time. After a few hours I bowed to popular opinion and we tacked north. It was still not a great course, but there was some north in it.

We were fighting our way up the west coast of Ireland in squally conditions when Jordan began to complain of severe stomach pains. For me, as skipper, this was a potentially serious problem. Could it be appendicitis? It did not seem to be hurting in the right place for that. How seriously should I take it? Constipation perhaps, 'Have you been going to the loo, Jordan?' 'Yes,' he said. 'Where does it hurt?' 'Sort of here.' I was rapidly coming to the conclusion that my first aid certificate was below par for emergencies such as this.

We had deliberately stayed a safe distance out to sea, well away from western Ireland's lee shore, but now, just in case, I studied the Imray charts to see if I could spot an easy approach to somewhere on the coast that might have a hospital. With strong tidal streams marked on the charts, and an unknown coastline, it all looked pretty complicated and there seemed no obvious place to head for. So we sailed on and I took over Jordan's watches – he needed little persuasion to take to his bunk and stay there.

Of course the weather then chose to get stormy again. I decided to experiment with a tactic that I was sure a friend of mine, Willy Ker, had told me he used in stormy weather on *Assent*, his celebrated Contessa 32. We beam reached across the seas with three reefs in the mainsail, but we were going too fast for comfort in such stormy conditions, and then as the depression went through and the wind backed we were driven farther and farther westward out into the Atlantic. Later Willy wrote, 'I was amused at your account of what you did in stormy conditions. What I actually do is take all sail down and beam reach a little upwind on the Aries self-steering.' The old rogue – but he is still a friend of mine (I think).

By the next morning we were a good distance offshore so we gybed to set a course more towards the coast. Jordan got up for a while for a blather, albeit conditions were still bouncy with non-stop and often very heavy rain. We held a course north-eastwards towards the north-west corner of Ireland. And here was a curious thing: the closer we got to land, the more Jordan seemed to recover. When we closed the land next morning he felt even better and as soon as he had mobile phone reception he was completely cured! John had always suspected that Jordan's stomach pain was psychosomatic, caused by the combined effects of the stress of a rather lively passage, living a very different life at sea from the one he was used to, and the fact that his mother was unwell. We were relieved to see Jordan recovered, although now he just drove us mad by chattering constantly on his mobile.

After all that it had blown, the wind died away completely as we rounded the north-west corner of Ireland. Now, when we were so keen to head across to the Scottish west coast, then up the Firth of Lorne and home, it was indeed frustrating to be virtually becalmed. In the end we took all sail down and drifted. In the evening the wind increased gradually and then came in to give us some glorious sailing: we barrelled along on the wind all through the night, past the lighthouse on Dubh Artach, in to the Firth of Lorne and so up towards Mull.

Some fluky airs in the lee of Mull turned to a strong, steady breeze which enabled us to charge up Loch Linnhe towards Port Appin.

But no sooner had we passed through the narrow channel by Castle Stalker than the wind died to nothing. With no engine to speak of, how were we going to get into the bay and onto our mooring? John had radioed his friend, Crawford, also out sailing that afternoon, and we recruited his help. So we suffered the final indignity of being towed to the pontoon at Lettershuna by Appin strapped alongside Crawford's boat and in full view of all.

03

ATLANTIC VARIANTS

Some went down to the sea in ships… He commanded, and raised the
stormy wind, which lifted up the waves of the sea. They mounted up to
heaven, they went down to the depths; their courage melted away…
Then they cried to the Lord in their troubles…

BOOK V, PSALM 107:25–26

The Atlantic can be very moody, and in its northern extremes completely unpredictable. Here are two passages I undertook, widely divergent voyages both in direction and character, both pioneering in their ways: the first straight across the Atlantic, for a purpose; the second an attempt to trace the early Viking settlers' search for new lands in what became the New World. Both were attempted with schoolboys and school leavers. But before I could embark on the transatlantic voyage, if I was to be entrusted with the lives of precious youth I needed to get some proper sailing qualifications under my belt.

'THE FIRST SCHOOL ACROSS THE ATLANTIC, AND BACK'

Two years after the first Azores passage, with pupils from Kingham Hill School and in the face of some opposition from the board of governors, I managed to put together an exploit, which I termed 'The First School across the Atlantic, and Back'*. It was a natural progression from the previous trip, it had not been done by a school and schoolboys before to my knowledge, and for me at least it was a chance to mark the school's centenary year, although some of the school governors and especially the chairman were not particularly happy about the idea. Perhaps the chairman didn't think the school should be involved in such activities, or there may even have been some personal antipathy – I really don't know, but he gave me a terrible grilling one evening at a meeting where it was pointedly discussed. Fairly, it was put to the vote at the end and a majority found in favour of the plan. Maybe this was what passed for risk assessment in those days.

One stipulation, as it had been for the earlier Azores trip, was that we should be vetted by a qualified and experienced sailor before we left. Geoff Hales, a friend and a Royal Yachting Association (RYA) examiner who had completed Observer Singlehanded Transatlantic Races (OSTARs) in 1976 and 1984, fitted the bill. He agreed to check us out and thus would sail with us from Portland, where I kept the boat, to Falmouth and put us through our paces. Will (who sailed with us in the 'Azores or Bust' voyage) had left the school by now and was returning to act as mate on this trip, steady and reliable as he was. So at Falmouth, both Will and I would take our RYA Yachtmaster Offshore qualification.

Our examiner was a short, wiry, ordered man, and with his huge experience was going to be tough to impress. I remember the 'blindfold' element being especially tricky; sitting down below, unable to see what was happening outside and using only compass, echo sounder, speed and estimated tidal flow in order to give the

---

* This was subtitled 'Portland UK to Portland USA' (Maine)

crew on deck directions to steer. No satellite navigation was allowed – in fact this was before the days of GPS. I was first in the hot seat, and the rest of the crew and Geoff were on deck. Slightly stressed admonitions were coming down from the crew above, 'St Anthony Head lighthouse coming up. And rocks are getting awfully close, Rev.' Somehow we scraped past. When it came to his turn Will, too, had a tough time 'blind' steering to a buoy up the Fal estuary. But we both passed.

Geoff said goodbye in Falmouth and the rest of us set sail for our first Atlantic crossing. As well as Will, our crew included two other Kingham Hill pupils: Rojo – small, wiry, keen to have a go – and Christian. My son Petey was at another school, but as he was my son I thought it acceptable he should join under our auspices. We made reasonable progress applying Geoff's mantra of close reaching on the 'making tack' when going to windward on an ocean passage – the 'making tack' being the one closest to the ideal course, directly upwind to your destination. I have followed this advice ever since, rather to the surprise of some of my crews who have probably thought we should be plugging a more direct course, hard against the wind. But why stress the boat and crew hammering against wind and sea when there is usually plenty of ocean to play with, the going is more comfortable and the boat goes faster?

Memories of this first Atlantic crossing are varied. Through the good offices of a Kingham parent the army had lent us a Clansman HF radio, powered by what would now seem rather large NiCad batteries. These we had to charge through a transformer from our own ship's batteries. The radio worked well to begin with and we communicated with the school via an RAF station in the north of Scotland, but after 500 miles or so it faded until eventually we lost communication altogether. This was no real problem for us, but the parents had expected updates and my poor wife had to field many anxious calls. Had she heard anything? 'No, but I am sure no news is good news and they're all right,' Kate would say.

We were blissfully unaware of this of course, but as we were approaching the coast of Newfoundland we came up with a coastguard cutter and despite feeling rather apprehensive about disturbing them with a personal request I called them up on the VHF and asked if there was any way they could put in a call to Britain for us. 'No problem, sir, we'll route it through St John's. Give us the number to ring,' and that was that. It was some months before I learned from Kate how relieved the parents had been to hear news of us and it made me realise that it is always more worrying for those waiting at home. So from then on, as we had no means in those days of reliably communicating home, we all agreed that no one would hear anything at all until we reached our destination. Better, we thought, to know you will hear nothing than to expect to hear something and become worried when you don't.

As no one had attempted what we were doing, and because we intended to claim a sailing first, we were again reluctant to use the engine. Thus for three days we were becalmed some distance off Newfoundland. We were treating it as a race, keen to set a time in case any other school should ever want to try and beat our record.

While we waited for wind the crew went swimming. I took pictures from the dinghy, ready to get back aboard at the first sign of any breeze. At last the tedium was broken, the breeze began to fill in and from a rather vague dead reckoning, not knowing our drift but feeling we must be nearing the coast, I tried fixing our position by shooting the moon and the sun together – a far cry from Captain Cook's or Joshua Slocum's lunar distances method, but it echoed something of the same principles.

But the moon moves very fast and the position from the computed crossed lines made little sense. Fortunately Cape Race at the southern end of Newfoundland soon hove in to sight and lived up to its name, with broken water and the crash of surf smashing onto rocks. We had officially crossed the Atlantic, but as we had planned to sail from Portland UK to Portland USA (Maine), the voyage was by no means over.

I still have a guilty conscience about the bad time I was giving Rojo, who was somehow becoming the butt of the party. As we ran down the coast of Nova Scotia I would make him steer another few minutes every time he lost the wind or gybed the main. I remember also giving him a rocket when he was up the mast and the bucket of tools he was carrying went spinning and crashing dangerously around. I hope I know better now, but at the time we were all still learning the art of living in close proximity on a small boat for weeks on end, where small things can become disproportionately large. He has forgiven me since!

In spite of mist and darkness and relying on dead reckoning – there was no sun to be seen for a sight – we managed to miss the reefs off notorious ship-killing Sable Island, but we did get caught by the ferocious tides at the south-west corner of Nova Scotia.

The Bay of Fundy, with the 'biggest tides in the world' and some of the strongest tidal streams, is just to the north. As the evening mist descended we were swept helplessly past an outer marker buoy and in among the numerous islands and shoals at the south-western tip of Nova Scotia. With no GPS to give us a position we spent a tense night navigating entirely by compass, echo sounder, good fortune and Radio Direction Finder (RDF).

The RDF was a curious instrument, looking rather like a ray gun, with a set of earphones which picked up the signals transmitted by radio beacons. The bearing of the beacon was established by swinging the gun back and forth until the signal was at its weakest, which seemed odd to me. What with the mist, tides and rudimentary ray gun we were never completely sure of where we were among the islands, or indeed where they were. At last the dawn came, which was a relief, but I suspect it was really the tide turning and spitting us out that got us free rather than any fine navigation on my part, and fortunately it did so in the direction of Maine and our final destination, Portland. We might make it after all.

After some confusion about immigration procedures, we headed for the Portland Yacht Club to the north and were directed to a mooring on the seaward side of the many yachts already there. We had arrived safely in America.

The hospitality of Americans is legendary – the yacht club showed us every kindness – and so is their appetite. I was taken out to dinner by our friend Gloria, the club secretary, and felt obliged to try an American T-bone steak. It was enormous and almost impossible to finish. Later a scion of the Hershey chocolate company lent us his Toyota van for the 300 mile round trip to Boston to fill our butane gas cylinders (cold winters freeze butane, so they only use propane in Maine). At the gas station I became convinced that the man behind the grill kept a revolver under the counter, just in case.

We were also given the key to the city of Portland at a Town Council Meeting. 'It might just buy you a cup of coffee somewhere in town,' said an American friend. We were interviewed by local TV journalists, who were especially interested in the reaction of boys barely out of school to sailing the Atlantic. Local people kindly had the new crew to stay in their homes until Rojo, Christian and Peter flew home. Peter had really only sailed with us to see America, but he now works in California where he has settled together with his partner, Danielle, and their recent baby boy.

The return passage

All too soon it was time to leave, and with some sadness we bade our farewells on the pontoon at the yacht club. The west-to-east passage is meant to be downwind, downhill, and for several days we made excellent progress with favourable winds, keeping well clear of the south coast of Nova Scotia and Sable Island this time. After twelve days we were virtually halfway across the Atlantic at around 30°W longitude.

Our crew for the return leg comprised Will, Steve (Dood), Ian (who was up for anything challenging) and Roger. My wife had done a splendid job with Roger, who had phoned her two weeks before he was due to come out to say that he was very apprehensive and didn't think he could do it. Kate persuaded him in her positive way, and now, schooled by Will, he was coping well. Soon after we arrived home Roger joined the Royal Marines, and has now risen from the ranks to be an officer. One good thing about sailing with those who have little previous experience is that they seem to accept it all and get on with it. That at least is what I took for granted, but nevertheless, thinking back, they must have coped magnificently in extremely difficult conditions. Adults might have been scared; youth and schoolboys just take it in their stride, as long as you yourself appear to be taking it as a matter of course. Or that is my experience, generally.

Mid-way across the wind began to head us. A huge high pressure system had developed over Europe and for the next twenty-three days we were hard on the wind. Twenty-three days against wind and sea – sheer torture. Moreover the wind was Force 5–8 most of the time. Under the watch system I was using at that time I was on permanent call and standby. In the days before roller reefing headsails it meant that I did all the changing of foresails on the foredeck, often swept by wind and sea. But the lads did the steering.

The navigation was down to me, too. I would hang on to a stay with one hand and shoot the sun holding the sextant with the other. Down below, in a bucking boat, the maths was an ordeal. With the advent first of Loran, then Satnav and then GPS I swiftly relaxed my opinion about electronic aids and am now delighted to be relieved of the daily chore of establishing a position from dead reckoning and 'shooting the sun', with its attendant maths. I still carry a sextant but I would have to read the books again if I ever had to use it in anger.

We crashed and banged to windward; sometimes when we fell off a big wave into the trough it sounded like an exploding artillery shell. One afternoon a sudden agonised yell erupted from the cockpit. Then silence. Dood later told us how a whale had appeared from nowhere and had shot towards the boat, diving under only at the last moment. No wonder he looked shaken.

After a while it began to look as if we might have to put in to La Coruña in Spain. The easterly was on the nose and driving us farther and farther south. At last the wind relented and allowed us to bear away north again. As we entered the Western Approaches another astro-navigation mix-up caused a moment or two of head scratching. The vital plus and minus signs had changed now we were farther north and I had forgotten about this. That wretched maths again. It may have thrown the calculations out somewhat; we certainly came rather too close to the Bishop Rock lighthouse that night for our peace of mind.

Later the Wolf Rock not so much howled but boomed obligingly as we passed. Then after days of wind we were becalmed, and we were already late for the start of term. Although we had been given some latitude by the governors I felt we had no alternative but to fire up the engine. That evening we ate our last full meal on board, which included one rusty, tired-looking tin of baked beans from the bilges. We celebrated having crossed the Atlantic both ways. We were late, but safely back.

After a brief stop in Falmouth and a lively thrash across Lyme Bay, we rounded Portland Bill and sailed into our home port of Weymouth, where the adventure had begun. The Royal Dorset Yacht Club feted us, and we scurried back to school as quickly as we could.

IN THE WAKE OF THE VIKINGS

Nothing ventured, nothing gained.
NJAL'S SAGA, ANONYMOUS, 13TH CENTURY

Two years passed before the next serious adventure. A pattern was emerging: on alternate years we would do a more adventurous expedition. We had done the Azores, we had done the Atlantic. What was next? The voyages of the Vikings up north seemed interesting and intriguing. Perhaps we could follow in their wake.

As before, the crew were all from Kingham Hill School. Howesy was chunky and apparently cheerful (but, as I discovered later, perhaps lacking in confidence) and Henchy was something of an extrovert, destined to join the Royal Engineers later. Both were about to leave the school and came on my later Antarctic expedition (*see* Antarctica and broke, page 66). Robin was quite a tall lad and perhaps a little out on a limb from the rest, as sometimes happens with schoolboys. Then there was Ian: tall, wiry and fit, and already a mountain man from being brought up in Nepal. He had recently left the school and was now returning to act as mate on this trip.

The school governors knew what we were intending to do, but this time, perhaps because I wrote a long justification and things had gone well previously, we were not subjected to an inquisition. Nor did we have to ask Geoff Hales for his services.

So far I have made fourteen Atlantic crossings, in my own and other people's boats, but this crossing was probably the most ambitious, involving island – and continent – hopping on the voyage out, and a direct transatlantic on the way back. In a number of ways it was as true a voyage of discovery for us as it had been for those early Scandinavian seafarers who had set out into the unknown in search of lands to cultivate.

The plan was to follow the Vikings' route across the north Atlantic, visiting the places they colonised as they pressed ever further westwards, reaching the American continent long before Christopher Columbus. But they had taken hundreds of years. Could we do it in a summer holiday?

We made our departure from Weymouth in June and school half-term found us plugging along the south coast of England against strong south-westerly winds. After turning north to Holyhead we left the boat on a mooring lent by the Holyhead Sailing Club. After the exams were finished we rejoined *Dodo* and called in at the Isle of

Man, once a Viking stronghold, then at Loch Ryan by Stranraer. It was there that disaster struck.

I had slipped away to Durham for my eldest daughter's graduation and while I was away the mooring strop chafed through and parted. In a desperate attempt to save the boat from drifting ashore the crew had started the engine and tried to motor to safety. In the process the propeller caught a rope and worse, when a fishing boat gave a tow, the propeller shaft had been wrenched out of the back of the gearbox. It was a weekend of course so everything was closed. The lads were understandably rather sheepish about the mishap and I wondered how seriously the damage was going to affect the expedition. Five days and a bucketful of cash later, the gearbox was fixed. In spite of the cost it was worth it; we could go. With relief we sailed out of Loch Ryan.

At least the wind had by now gone round to the south, and for me there began an island passage of some romance. Folklore and history wafted by on every shore, from Robert Louis Stevenson's *Kidnapped* and Compton Mackenzie's *Whisky Galore* to Somerled and the Vikings, the Scottish Lords of the Isles, Stevenson lighthouses and the wrecks of the Spanish Armada.

In the early morning we sailed past the Mull of Kintyre and Islay with its mighty tidal rips and soon, to starboard, we could see Iona, a beautiful island and the cradle of Celtic Christianity in Scotland. The slanting coastlines of Tiree and Coll gave way to a long hard night-sail past the Isle of Canna to Skye. And then the wind gave out – here, of all places, in the traditionally storm-tossed Minches, and we had to resort to the engine. Clearing the Butt of Lewis that evening, the wind came in and increased from the west and south, giving us a fine if energetic run past the deserted island of North Rona somewhere out there to the west in the dark, and so up to Suderoy, the southernmost of the Faroe Islands.

The Faroes

The vertiginous cliffs and headlands of the Faroes are both barren and beautiful; the sea cliffs are the highest in Europe and the tidal currents among the strongest. When we sighted the islands we were so pleased with ourselves that we gave no thought to the terrific speed at which we were approaching them and, in thick mist, we overshot the entrance to the fjord we were looking for. And we were about to find out why … as soon as we turned around we realised the tide was running at a ferocious rate of knots: sailing against it was out of the question and even under engine it took us a good two hours to cover the mile or so back to the fjord's entrance.

Our stay in the Faroes was all too brief. The people are of Viking descent and the Nordic influence is apparent today in their language, architecture and, one might say, character. The Faroese supplied Britain with fish during the Second World War and an elderly fisherman I met on the quayside told how out of four boats fishing off Iceland during the war his was the only one to return; the others were all sunk by U-boats. Then a young deep-sea trawler skipper showed us around his boat and I was surprised to learn how highly competitive the industry is. There were two of everything on the bridge, just in case.

While the islanders appeared to be naturally quiet people it appeared the favoured form of entertainment for the younger generation was driving nowhere in particular at breakneck speed. The crew returned ashen faced after being taken for a 'fearful ride' one night.

Three days later it was time say goodbye and we slipped out of Tveraa (Tvøroyri) harbour in the middle of the night. It was soon daylight and the tide was with us this time as we tacked past colossal headlands and rounded the north of the island. I mistook a deep inlet for open sea but the radar saved the day and we settled down to sail a direct course towards Iceland.

After two easy days' cruising in sun and fair winds the wind began to rise, and by the time it had reached a strong Force 8–9 we were flying the storm jib alone. Torrential rain flattened the sea and to some extent our spirits as, peering through the blown spume, we sped through the night. The sea was lively and rough but not threatening and the crew took it in their stride, steering as best they could towards Iceland, peering through the murk, but still doing single watches on their own, and coping without complaint.

In 1973 a volcano erupted on the island of Heimaey in the Vestmannaeyjar archipelago and the inhabitants sprayed sea water onto the advancing lava flows in a desperate effort to keep their main harbour entrance open. They succeeded, but only just, and I had no intention of attempting the very narrow entrance in a storm. We continued south until morning when an island to starboard spurred a detour, 'Quick,' I yelled, 'let's tack and take a look.' The crew put in the tack, but they looked puzzled, muttering that it was only a lump of land. But this lump of land, I explained, was Surtsey, which erupted out of the sea in 1963 and was, therefore, the newest lump of land on God's good earth. Surtsey fascinated me. It looked almost completely barren, an island of black volcanic rock and dust that had been on the map for only twenty-five years.

From here we carried on northwards to pass Reykjanes, the south-westerly point of Iceland, where the tides do strange things and an isolated rock in the shape of a sabre tooth juts out of the sea. Thousands of wheeling, diving, skimming sea birds peppered the air around us and one of them perched awhile on Ian's head – fearless. On land, jets of steam spurted from volcanic fissures – from a distance they looked like miniature tornados. We would be in Reykjavik, the capital of Iceland, by morning.

Iceland

For us, Iceland was most memorable not for its landscape or its people, but for how very expensive everything was. A tourist brochure confirmed that the country, in those days, had the 'highest cost of living in Europe' and the city dwellers here appeared well-heeled, sophisticated and to be enjoying the good life. We eked out our budget over three days, but any longer would have seen us broke, and school leavers aren't flush with cash anyway.

The weather bureau's charts showed that there was still ice around Cape Farewell at the southern tip of Greenland, but the weather looked favourable. We deliberated for a while, decided to go for it and next day we sailed gently out of Reykjavik on a light breeze. We had not gone far down the course when the wind settled in more strongly from the east and north-east and, sails goosewinged, we were soon running hard downwind. It was only then that I realised my homemade pole (holding out the headsail) weighed a ton and required nearly all hands to rig it.

Meanwhile whales and porpoises came swimming with the boat; the whales spouted and the porpoises gambolled playfully around and in front of the boat as they do. In Iceland, seabirds had been the predominant wildlife, but here in the Denmark Strait between Iceland and Greenland it was certainly the creatures of the deep. We had marine mammals in abundance. We passed only one ship, a large trawler that seemed to have a somewhat forbidding air. I radioed and after a stony silence came a peremptory exchange. I like to think that it might have been a Russian spy ship.

The wind strengthened and headed us as we approached Cape Farewell. I was wondering how many reefs to put in the mainsail when the decision was ripped out of my hands: the sail had torn in two. Changing the mainsail, beam on to a big sea and rolling around in a strong Force 6–7, was extremely difficult. Between us we had to extract the slides from the luff groove in the mast, unshackle the clew from the end of the boom and unreeve the reefing lines, at the same time as wrestling the unruly bunt of loose sail down onto the deck in the wind. Then we had to repeat the process in reverse with the new sail, with it all still rolling and blowing.

We shall never forget that evening. The wind had moderated and we were under headsail and the spare mainsail. All of a sudden, as the mist gradually lifted to reveal the high snow-capped mountains of Greenland, we saw, for the first time floating majestically towards us on the wind, icebergs and growlers. It was an unforgettable experience seen from the deck of our small and vulnerable boat.

We were not nearly so euphoric the next day, however, when the mist descended again and we spent the entire day dodging ice. It certainly concentrated the mind and it was here that our new black-and-white radar came into its own. One of us sat down below watching the screen and shouting up 'starboard now' or 'port a bit now' to the helmsman, who weaved between growlers and bergy bits and bigger bergs. We were almost totally reliant on the radar. A friend of mine who has sailed a lot in the Arctic used to say, 'Men don't need radar'. Some years later he had changed his tune, and there is no doubt we had cause to be grateful for its guiding hand that day.

We broke free later that day and at dusk found ourselves struggling to decide which fjord would lead us into Julianehäb (or Qaqortoq as it is known today). Which of these fjords is the right one? Suddenly I saw a light flashing in the distance. I leapt down below and scanned the chart and rushed back on deck, 'It's all right now, lads, steer for the light.' The light was a beacon marked on the chart at the end of the fjord leading to Qaqortoq, so we were able to close the port quite easily and tie up against the jetty.

We collapsed into our bunks and when we woke next morning we found we were hanging off our mooring lines from the quayside. I had not allowed enough slack for the big tides of Greenland. The jamming hitches I had put in the line were impossible to undo and in the end I had to cut the rope. The boat slid back down onto an even keel. Never again will I put jamming hitches on mooring lines.

Greenland

Greenland was stark, barren, desolate, uncompromising but strangely beautiful, its long fjords filled with ice breaking off the glaciers moving down from the Greenland ice cap. On the other hand the life of the people was generally relaxed and apparently unregulated. There were no nasty things like customs officers to greet you on arrival nor any need to obtain a gun license if you carried a firearm. Guns could even be bought over the counter in any supermarket. Unregulated and relaxed it may have been, but the first question asked of Robin when he got off the boat was, 'Got any grass?' Admittedly Robin at the time did look a bit as if he might have some.

We could not help noticing that most of the Inuit population seemed to be living on welfare and Carlsberg, their old way of life destroyed, especially here in the south of the country. Was it the malign influence of Western culture?

Back on the Viking trail we motored up Eiriksfjord through glacier ice to anchor near a sizeable iceberg, which we hoped was grounded and unlikely therefore to move, before walking over the hill along the old Kings' Way to Igaliko (Gardar) to inspect the ruins of the ancient Norse cathedral and bishop's house. Huge stones and ruins stood in a well-ordered pattern on a beautiful flat plain by the sea.

The Norse, as the Vikings became known in Greenland, brought their Christianity and culture with them, which marked them apart from the Inuit. What a pity they did not also adopt the Inuit way of life, living off the sea and land instead of relying almost entirely on farming. The Norse might then have survived rather than mysteriously disappearing from Greenland some 400 years later.

Erik the Red 'discovered' this new land in the tenth century, and in a clever marketing ploy to entice potential colonists he named it Green Land. To be fair it was warmer then and consequently a little more fertile. Back in the fjord, we met up with the crew of the German yacht *Freydis* and its Viking-mad skipper at the site of Brattahlid, Erik's ancient homestead, which we explored together. Here, the first church in the western hemisphere had been built by Erik the Red's wife, although she was obliged to build it down a slope so her non-Christian husband need not see it. In the homestead's cattle stalls a whale's shoulder blade formed one of the divisions, and by the shore we visited the remains of ancient Inuit turf dwellings. To keep in the heat they were built with tiered floors and low entrances, with layers of turf interspersed with rows of stone, creating a sound, insulating foil against the cold. We crawled in and, imagining the turf structure was still there, thought how tight space must have been for the occupants.

Greenland and its people fascinated me. Our time here was too short to gain much insight, but long enough for me to know I must go back. I vowed to return.

For a more contemporary flavour of Greenland we motored across the fjord to look around the airfield at Narsarsuaq airport from where one of the Danish Meteorological Institute's sea-ice monitoring bases, Ice Central, had supplied information to mariners since the late 1950s. Before the advent of satellite technology, data was gathered by aircraft flying over the Greenland Waters area, which made the whole process rather slow by comparison.

The time had come to return to Qaqortoq to prepare for the next long passage. On the way southwards we put out fishing lines one night and immediately hooked in to a shoal of cod. By the time we had eaten our way through our catch, and it took days, we reckoned we had begun to look like cod.

At Qaqortoq an elderly Inuit man who had once been a sea captain repaired our torn mainsail on what was reputed to be the 'only Singer sewing machine in Greenland'. On the old man's workshop wall hung a rack with fifteen hunting rifles neatly stacked and ready for the winter seal and walrus season. Sitting for hours by a little hole in the ice waiting to harpoon their prey is not for modern-day hunters. It is quicker, safer and easier for the hunter to find a seal basking on the ice then, hidden behind a white cloth he pushes slowly ahead of him, to shoot his quarry from a distance.

In the light of gale warnings we delayed our departure from Qaqortoq for two days which allowed us to meet up with a couple from Norway whom we had first come across in Reykjavik aboard their boat *Trude*. Then, because it had an English name, we noticed a boat lifted out on shore. Its French/Italian owners told how, during the preceding summer in a storm off Cape Farewell, they had been rolled over three times and on the third roll the boat had been dismasted. 'And we have still never seen Cape Farewell,' they cried. The new mast had been shipped to Qaqortoq and they were there to supervise it being stepped. 'But we won't do it on Monday,' they said. 'Friday is payday so everyone will have hangovers on Monday.' They were already wise to Greenland's heavy drinking culture since during the winter someone, to their dismay, had opened up their steering compass and drunk all the alcohol from inside the bowl.

The forecast was still for strong wind, but we set sail in light airs for Labrador and Newfoundland. We had a cracking passage and in a mere five and a half days we had reached the Canadian coast. The icebergs on this side of the Davis Strait were bigger than any we had encountered before, and on one beautiful sunny morning there appeared a majestic iceberg with a prominent arch hollowed out at its centre. It was too good a photo opportunity to miss. 'Pump up the dinghy,' I ordered. 'Robin, you drive it. Ian, go with him, you can take the pictures.' Howesy, Henchy and I stayed on board and motored towards the iceberg, keeping *Dodo*'s sails up for the camera. Ian took some shots of us approaching the berg, then keen to get *Dodo* framed in the huge arch now hidden from us, I motored closer to the cold, gleaming ice and began to round it. A loud, sharp crack sounded. 'I don't like this,' I said, and edged out a little. Silence. All was well. I relaxed, steered the boat in past a huge pillar of ice at one corner, set her up for the picture and Ian snapped the shutter.

Dinghy and crew were aboard and we had started to move away. As I threw a backward glance at the berg the huge ice pinnacle we had just rounded collapsed into the sea. The momentum of many tons of ice fired the frozen hulk like a missile through the water we had barely cleared. Then it slowed and came to rest, wallowing in the sea.

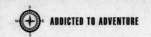

We left in sober mood and chastened. We had learned never to mess about with icebergs.

Later that day a new frontal system brought the wind direction we needed to sail through isolated icebergs towards Belle Isle. There, as we were sailing between two large icebergs not far offshore and one further out, a huge gust of wind overpowered the boat. Was it affected by the icebergs? Do icebergs make their own weather? I don't know, but first we heard and then we saw the cruising chute starting to tear across its top. 'Quick, get it down,' I yelled. The crew flashed about the decks; a quick release of the halyard before rapidly hauling armfuls of sail, yard upon yard, out of the water. They had managed to save it from serious damage. Robin meanwhile had slept down below through all the noise and confusion. Though this may have raised a few eyebrows among the rest of us, with hindsight this was fair enough, as he was off watch and was doing the right thing catching up on sleep.

We sailed smoothly past the end of this rocky, inhospitable island, but halfway across the Strait of Belle Isle, in a dying breeze and gathering darkness, we put the engine on and motored through the passage into the enclosed inlet of Quirpon. Forgetting to allow for the different scale of the new chart, I went too far in and we were brought up short on a sandbank. I reversed quickly and was about to call for the anchor to go down to sort things out in the morning when a dory came streaming out from the shore with a youngster at the wheel shouting, 'I saw youz from my sitting room window, and I saiz "there'z a man who doesn't know where he'z going".' He led us to the wharf, as he called it. 'Theyz usually puts that loight on but it's orff tonoight.' Welcome to Newfoundland.

Newfoundland

Newfoundland was quite a place. I got up early to take on fresh water and filled the ship's tank from a hose on the wharf. As I finished topping up a lad ambled over and said, 'Oi doin't suppoise it matters that there'z sarlt water, doez it?' So not all hoses on wharfs deliver fresh water? Not in Newfoundland's fishing hamlets apparently. We had to wait until we reached the town of St Anthony some days later before we could pump it all out and refill the tank with fresh water, and the 'sarlt' we pumped out had done no good at all to the Aquafilter we had in our water system.

From Quirpon we threaded carefully through rocky passages round to Epaves Bay to visit L'Anse aux Meadows, the only excavated Viking site in the New World. As in Greenland, a frisson of the Viking spirit rose within us when we anchored off the beach where the settlers must have landed 1000 years before; we felt sharply in touch with this earlier civilisation as we rowed ashore and walked where the Norse had walked those centuries earlier.

At L'Anse aux Meadows excavations by Norwegian archaeologists and Canada Parks have proven beyond doubt that the Norse settled here. In addition to the remains of many of the dwellings, and precise full-size reconstructions of three of the turf longhouses, the visitor centre is packed with the stuff of the Norsemen's daily life. So was this where the great early explorer 'Lucky' Leif Erikson spent his winter in Vinland? Probably. And later it may also have served as a valuable resting place for those venturing farther into the wilds of North America.

In strong wind and rain we motored back to Quirpon, out through the narrow channel at its southern end to open sea, and south to the little fishing hamlet of Griguet. Sailor, writer and broadcaster Tom Cunliffe spent time here in 1983 on his Bristol Channel pilot cutter *Hirta* where, villagers included, a very good time was had by all. Friendships had been forged and the people of Griguet remembered well the music, song and dance they had enjoyed on board with Tom and his crew. I know Tom, and thus we found ourselves basking in the reflected sunshine of his visit. I had a copy of his book *Topsail & Battleaxe* aboard which recounts *Hirta*'s voyage from England to northern Newfoundland, in which some of the villagers we met are featured by name, much to their delight. One man, Alan Loder, a park warden at 'Lancey Meadows' as the settlement site was known locally, was training to be a Pentecostal minister and had built himself a sailing boat in only fourteen days; he had also made an intricately detailed model of *Hirta*. Alan was a great help, later driving us around to collect diesel and stores. We would have been stuck without him.

Time was moving on apace and, even now, if the wind turned against us we would be late for the beginning of term – again. There was always that pressure with school trips. After a rather unfamiliar, to me, Pentecostal service at Alan's church in St Anthony we ticked off our final checks, scrubbed the weed off *Dodo*'s waterline and, in the afternoon, motored out past St Anthony's Light. An hour or so later I killed the engine and, once more, we settled down to sail the Atlantic.

Atlantic return

Our spirits were soon raised by the sight of icebergs brought south on the Labrador current, glistening in the afternoon sunshine. Then, striking eastwards, a beautiful sunset silhouetted our last glimpse of land to the west. From here my memories become rather jumbled and confused, probably because the passage left little time for reflection. The wind blew strongly, first from the north for three or four days, and then switched to the south; both directions gave us fast beam reaching. And then in mid-Atlantic in the middle of the night it really started to blow, a full gale.

Conditions called for reduced sail. I was at the bow, changing down from the No. 3 jib to the storm jib (we still did not have roller reefing, and I was still doing all the foredeck work) with the boat roaring along when a big sea picked up the stern and the helmsman crash gybed. Back in the cockpit Ian pointed silently to the boom. It was bent at 20–30 degrees where the line for the third reef met the aft end of the boom. We would have to sail half the Atlantic with a bent boom. There was no other way. The boom, however, seemed strong enough and the bend did not seriously alter the shape of the mainsail which, in any case, was reefed most of the time. When the boom was accidentally gybed again (conditions *were* stormy) it held. The perpetrator did however get a rocket from the skipper, which I think in the circumstances was justified, though I do try to keep such to a minimum.

Things were going well. The wind stayed consistently strong but we were reaching or running before, which was a bonus. There was none of that beating to windward with all its banging and crashing that had been such a persistent trial on our previous crossing. Spirits remained high and the crew began to keep a record, ticking off the days with guesstimates of how long the passage was going to take posted up on the bulkhead. The final days as we entered sea region Sole were exhilarating, running before strong following winds with clouds visible on the horizon over southern Ireland. My abiding memory is of Howesy on watch hunched over the wheel, muttering to himself as he wrestled with a Force 6–7 and a big following sea, no doubt rightly blaming the skipper for carrying too much sail. Then the first sighting of Sound Island Light on the Scilly Isles closely followed by the Bishop Light, and that final glorious run down past Round Island in the night, checking the radar to keep outside the line of rocks. Rosy-tinted clouds formed a backdrop to our run down to Wolf Rock in the early dawn. The wind, after blowing itself out for a while, returned. As we approached Lizard Point a Customs Cutter ranged alongside and radioed us. Half choking on a breakfast mouthful of scrambled egg, my reply must have sounded rather garbled.

Rounding the Lizard, past the Manacles buoy, we arrived off Falmouth. Under engine in the harbour, while avoiding one of those lovely Falmouth oyster-dredgers out racing on an August bank holiday, the trailing log caught round the prop. Once we were safely tied up close to the Customs Cutter, Robin dived to retrieve both line and spinner. Did they think we had concealed packages under the keel? Suspicious? Clearly not: they even invited us on board to shower, and gave us tea and biscuits.

St Anthony's Light, Newfoundland to St Anthony's Light, Falmouth in under fifteen days. We were 'well pleased' as my crew would say, and it was my fastest crossing ever. And, back in Weymouth, we made it for the beginning of term, just.

04

DEEP SOUTH; FAR NORTH

Antarctica has this mythic weight. It resides in the collective unconscious of so many people, and it makes this huge impact, just like outer space. It's like going to the moon.

FROM AN INTERVIEW WITH JOHN KRAKAUER,
AUTHOR AND MOUNTAINEER

Its overwhelming beauty touches one so deeply that it's like a wound.
BEYOND THE FROZEN SEA, EDWIN MICKLEBURGH

Cold has never been uppermost in my mind when planning a trip, and yet there are times when even the hardiest would swap everything for a warm bed. Of all my adventures, perhaps the hardest have been when cold has been a dominating factor. Curiously, during the two trips we made to Antarctica in 1994, the biggest challenge we had to face was not the weather but the loss of the mast. Cold, however, was to be our constant companion on a subsequent climbing trip to Greenland in

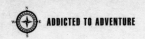

2004. And it was there, during a dark Arctic winter, alone on *Dodo's Delight*, that disaster struck.

ANTARCTICA AND BROKE

It was 1992, and I was newly retired from Kingham Hill School. Although I was sad to leave a school to which I had given so much energy, early retirement had many advantages, notably the time to plan a really ambitious expedition. A round-the-world voyage seemed like a good idea, as we had done a lot in the Atlantic Ocean already and this might be the culmination of all these expeditions so far. It would have to be via Antarctica and Cape Horn, of course, being ex-Royal Marines and addicted to challenge. Next came months of planning and fundraising, with which I was helped enormously by Heather McMullen, a Royal Cruising Club member who lived nearby and had taken an increasing interest in our proposed voyage. By early autumn the following year we were ready to set sail.

We left Falmouth on 15 September, 1993. There were five of us aboard: Steve (Dood), Simon (Pebs or Pebble – his brother in the SAS being known as Brick), Barnaby (Barney) and Ian – all former Kingham Hill pupils – and myself. Steve was by now an experienced sailor and had also trained and worked as a boatbuilder. He had already assumed the role of Mate, really by natural selection. Today I particularly admire the fact that though heavily dyslexic he has passed exams to gain a Master's ticket, and is the professional skipper of a superyacht. Simon was a laid back, charming character. Barnaby was our cockney, and was slightly ill at ease till we reached Rio de Janeiro – 'it's alright now, Rev, I've found a McDonalds.' Ian, the son of a Bishop, was our smoothy with slicked back hair and an eye for the girls, and has since become the professional skipper of a large Dutch yacht. Before we started Bishop Mike Whinney gave us a Service of Blessing with parents and friends on the pontoon by the Royal Cornwall Yacht Club, a fitting and pleasant occasion.

We had all sailed together before and quickly established a watchkeeping routine, as well as taking turns to do a day's cooking. At first we had a separate washing up rota, but it only led to disagreements: 'Surely you didn't need to use all those pans cooking?' was an early refrain. Thereafter, 'He who cooks, washes up' became the rule.

Via Madeira and the Canaries and on to the Cape Verde islands ('milk run' stuff), we crossed the equator to Rio de Janeiro. Of the passage a few memories stand out: the violent thunderstorms off the coast of Brazil with simultaneous lightning and loud thunder claps (meaning it was right overhead and lightning could strike the boat), a frightening experience as it was completely out of our control. Also tricky was trying to find a way through the long fishing nets that stretched for miles across the surface off the coast of Brazil. In Rio that huge statue of Christ the Redeemer impressed us all, all that is except young Barney, who was more impressed with the McDonald's.

But neither the statue of Christ nor McDonald's would keep us long in Rio because the crew were desperate to reach the Falklands for Christmas. In the Roaring Forties the wind truly became roaring, but by now the crew were well experienced and handled it as a matter of course. We made landfall on the night of 19 December and as we were tying up to the Town Quay at Port Stanley, my cousin, Dick Sawle, turned up to welcome us. He and his wife and family live on the islands in Port Stanley, and Dick ran a company called Polar, heavily involved with the fishing industry off the Falklands. The Customs Officer also came by to charge us £40 as an entry fee.

On Christmas Day we all trooped off to the cathedral in Port Stanley, after which the crew went to the dogs... Let me explain. Under the terms of the Antarctic Treaty, huskies are not considered to be indigenous and because of this a number were about to be transported to Canada. We had been allowed to see them where they were being kept, up the hill behind Stanley, before they were shipped out. Since humans are also a non-indigenous species, but not banned by the treaty, there seems little sense in banning huskies; surely they must be better than skidoos?

While in Stanley we also took the chance to renew the stainless steel eyes supporting the aft lower standing rigging wires (vital components in supporting the mast) at deck level. One of the eyes had burst on our way down the coast of Brazil and from then on we had sailed rather gingerly with a big U bolt fixed through the deck in its place, favouring the other tack where possible.

As a former Royal Marine, albeit of ancient vintage, it seemed appropriate to visit San Carlos. To leave without seeing where the British Task Force landed in 1982 was unthinkable, so at 0530 on 31 December we slipped our lines from the Town Pier and set out, closely pursued by the *James Clark Ross*, the Antarctic survey vessel which was heading down first to Mare Harbour and then on to South Georgia for a month. Feeling rather envious of them – we were not going to have time to visit South Georgia ourselves – we exchanged greetings by radio before going our separate ways.

After so many miles as a crew, the pattern for the short passage soon established itself, until 0600 the next morning, when one of the deck eyes astern burst abruptly out of the deck, leaving a hole big enough to allow water to pour onto the feet of the two crewmen sleeping in the aft cabin. Earlier we had attached both the sheets for the jib and the trysail through blocks to this eye at the stern and the combined strain had obviously proved too much for it. The problem now was how to repair it.

We hove-to, backing the jib, and I tried pushing sealant around the hole before pressing a section of wood hard down over the top, hoping it would stick and plug the hole. This worked for a while, but the deck was wet, the sealant did not adhere properly and the wood soon came away. We next resorted to shoving a plastic bin bag up through the hole, which did manage to stem most of the flow. Fortunately the crew in the aft cabin had stuffed themselves into their military-quality Gore-tex bivy bags to keep from getting soaked. By now it was also cold enough for the watchkeepers to climb into their Henri Lloyd survival suits, worn partly inflated for warmth. And, as it turned out, this was the suits' only outing on the entire circumnavigation.

Past the twin summits of Fanning Head we reached into San Carlos Water. Puffing pig porpoises swam alongside to greet us as we left the large Admiralty buoy abeam and the smaller wreck buoy, which marked the final, poignant resting place of HMS *Antelope* sunk in the Falklands War. We sailed into Pony's Valley Creek (where 40 Commando RM had landed in 1982), anchored, and crashed out in our bunks.

Pebs had a special, personal reason for visiting the war memorial at San Carlos. His father, a sergeant in the SAS, was killed during the war when a helicopter with some thirty SAS troopers aboard crashed into the sea shortly after take off from their ship. We went ashore and read the columns of names on the memorial wall and Sergeant Atkinson's was there among the others. It was a Sunday. We stood together by the memorial, I said a brief prayer and started to read a poem Pebs had brought with him. As I began to read the words I choked up and Pebs had to take over. It was a memorable and unashamedly emotional occasion for all of us as we remembered all those lives sacrificed.

We returned to Stanley and not only dealt with the deck eye and some repairs to the bow roller but also helped our friends cut their peats for the winter – heavy work, but it was an interesting experience, hefting the traditional spade and other cutting implements used down the generations.

At 0655 on 16 January we took in our mooring warps from the Town Pier and, leaving Wolf Rock to starboard, we headed southwards bound for Antarctica under a sunny sky. Barney and Ian had left the boat in Stanley and the ship's log records that our two replacement crew members, Henchy and Howesy, were having contrasting experiences. One was shaking down fast, '1500 Nice weather, nice food, what more can a man ask for?' The other may not have been quite so happy, '2100 I hope the Musto man feels better tomorrow', a reference both to the expensive foul-weather gear he had bought for the trip and to his seasickness.

Musto man's spirits soon rose; morale aboard was increasing, '0300 Good wind and enjoyable sailing ... 1100 Big waves, big birds, small boat.' It continued like this for three days as we sailed south-west across Drake Passage. The wind swung to the north for a while, the glass dropped, the wind died, then came back again more from the south-west. We turned more southwards. The temperature – air and sea – began to fall. 19 January, '0800 Water Temp 7°C ... 2210 Water Temp 5°C.' 20 January, '0500 Man, it's freezing!' And so it went on, down to 3°C, with the wind making it all feel colder. '1500 Cold, wet! But I love it ... 1600 Trysail and No. 3 jib.'

Next morning the skipper's plaintive entry in the log read, '0700 I don't know where the Antarctic Convergence was, but I think we must be past it. It's freezing! Water 2°C.' Taking into account the wind-chill factor again it felt very cold indeed. Drake Passage has a fearsome reputation for high winds and vertiginous seas so it was strange to be Trade-wind sailing – albeit in bitter cold – towards Antarctica, with two headsails poled out either side.

That evening, Dood pointed up at something I had noticed but not really seen for what it was: strands in both aft lower rigging wires were beginning to unravel where they went in to the Talurit fitting hooked into the mast. We winched Dood up to the spreaders in a bosun's chair and rigged 12mm safety lines alongside both shrouds and tensioned them up hard with block and tackle. In hindsight, this may have lulled us into a false sense of security.

Towards Cape Melville on the south-east corner of King George Island we passed close by the first large iceberg we had seen in the Southern Hemisphere. As we turned the corner and sailed along the south coast the sun burned off the mist from the adjoining peaks and ice cliffs; cape petrels and giant southern petrels soared above the boat while two humpback whales swam lazily by. We debated whether to go in to Admiralty Bay for the night but decided it was a little too early and sailed on in the rising wind, past another big iceberg, and into Maxwell Bay.

In Antarctica we had expected to find only isolation, remoteness, solitude; in fact Maxwell Bay turned out to be very crowded. No fewer than six or seven Antarctic national bases litter its shores – Argentinean, Chilean, Chinese, Korean, Russian, you name it. Everyone seemed to be here.

In order to avoid civilisation's unwelcome intrusion we tried to anchor away from the bases. This led to all sorts of minor dramas – trying to get our anchor to hold was far from easy owing to the incredibly steep-to shores in this glacial world. Eventually, forced to abandon our craving for solitude, we motored across the bay and dug our hook in near the Chinese and Chilean bases. Sheltered in the bay with no ice around, there was no need to set an anchor watch so – something of a treat – the whole crew enjoyed a peaceful, unbroken night's sleep.

The day dawned sunny with a light breeze. All seemed well and, without due thought, we set sail for the sheltered and reputedly well-protected haven of Yankee Harbour where we planned to fix the lower rigging wires which we had temporarily jury rigged before. It was a pleasant enough sailing day and we were just able to make the course across the mouth of Nelson Strait to Robert Island. During the night, although it was still light, the wind backed more westerly and freshened a little so we had to tack. At 0400 on 24 January, 10 miles from Yankee Harbour, in only 18–20 knots of wind and a moderate sea, we fell off a small wave. There was a loud bang, the starboard aft lower wire snapped and so did the safety line, and the mast fell over the side.

I was convinced we must have hit a rock and rushed on deck only to see 10 feet of the mast sticking up out of the water. Thoughts flashed through my mind. Was this the end of our voyage? Could we effect a repair? On the positive side, it was light and sunny. We surveyed the damage and pondered the options. 'Cut it all away,' cried Pebs, but the frugal side of me said no and we set about saving as much as we could. The wreckage of mast and sails was now half floating alongside to windward and acting as a kind of sea anchor – impossible to haul aboard. We checked there were no lines or rigging tangled in the prop and managed to motor the boat 180 degrees around, then, by locking the wheel right over, kept the wreckage downwind. Now, with the wreckage to leeward, we could work on it: unbolt shrouds, slacken halyards, take off the boom and rod kicker – both somehow still half on board – and haul the genoa and mainsail out of the water, along with all the rigging and, finally, both halves of the mast. I was thankful I had four strapping lads on board. It was all a terrible mess, but at least everything was back on deck. One of the jagged mast sections had scraped the topsides a bit but, thankfully, it hadn't punctured the hull.

Only then did we start to take pictures – not only as evidence for the insurance claim, but also because Henri Lloyd had asked for shots of their gear in extreme conditions: we reckoned this qualified.

I tried motoring on towards Yankee Harbour but with the engine alone we struggled to make much progress against wind and sea. Instead, we cut across the wind into English Strait and Discovery Bay to anchor – difficult, again, because of the depths – off the Chilean Antarctic naval base of Arturo Prat. The Chileans led us to an enclosed bay behind their base, though this did also involve running smack into a rock on the way. They then helped us ferry the wreckage ashore in a small cutter, with the two mast sections balanced precariously across our little rubber dinghy. With these we realised we could make a jury rig and now Dood, who had worked as a boatbuilder, took charge: he sawed off the jagged, broken end of the mast's bottom half, then took off the intact top section and bolted that on to the bottom half.

Our new mast, 18 feet in all, was just under half the length of the original. We got it back to the boat and by attaching ropes and with all five of us pushing and heaving, managed to raise it. With the mast in position we could more easily measure and cut down the standing rigging that would hold it up – although taking accurate measurements with a bendy tape measure was tricky and there were a few mistakes. With no Talurit press to hand (a machine for clamping the fitting onto the wire) we had to form eyes in the shrouds with bulldog clips and this, I thought, might be a point of weakness but there was no alternative. Three bulldog clips were put to each eye.

The Chilean navy lent us tools, repaired our outboard motor and even fed us for a few days. Antarctic bases have their own work to do; they're not there to rescue beleaguered mariners, yet the Chileans could not have done more for us and we were extremely grateful. Generous as they were by nature I think this may also have had something to do with Chile's long standing affinity with Britain. We had to decline an offer from a Chilean naval rescue ship to sink its stern, winch us aboard and then let the yacht fall on its side when the tide went out, or so we understood it. The charge would be $6,000, reduced from $10,000 after we had appealed on the grounds of poverty. It was then that I decided that if Shackleton could sail to safety across a stormy stretch of the Southern Ocean in a leaky old boat like the *James Caird*, we could surely do it in a well-found yacht like *Dodo's Delight*. Despite misgivings from Howesy – whom we simply taunted with echoes of his cry, 'We're gonna die. We're all gonna die' – we headed out under jury rig, into the Drake Passage, bound back towards the Falklands.

Straight away we noticed that, without the full mast to counterbalance the weight of the keel, the boat's motion was unpredictable, quick and jerky; after a while only the mate felt well enough to mock the rest of us. I was convinced that our jury rig would only allow us to jog along at 2–3 knots and we were bound to get clobbered somewhere between Antarctica and South America – a stretch of water notorious for storms and big seas. However, by hanking the No. 1 jib onto the forestay on its side (i.e. the foot became the luff or front of the sail) then sheeting it right back to a block on the stern cleat – 'windsock sailing', the crew called it – plus hoisting

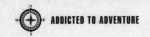

the trysail as a small main to help steady us, we found to our surprise that we could still sail at 4 or 5 knots and even 6 and more when the waves picked us up surfing.

It turned out to be a remarkable passage and, despite having to heave-to for a night and a morning mid-passage when the wind headed us, I still cannot work out how we made such good progress. We had nothing more than Force 8 touching 9 and although on one occasion we were knocked almost horizontal by a freak wave, with the preponderance of keel over mast weight we were up again so quickly we hardly had time to notice. Fortunately the winds in this part of the world are predominantly from south-west through to north-west, so we were either reaching or running virtually all the way, holding a diagonal course across Drake Passage towards the Falklands. Indeed, on days when the wind was on our aft quarter we were even surfing. It took us only a little over seven days to cover the 730 or so miles to the Falklands. 'Perhaps we should always sail with a jury rig,' I said, 'provided we don't have to go to windward.' I was only joking.

The ensuing few weeks in the Falklands were pretty stressful with much to organise, from sorting out insurance to arranging for all the gear we needed to be sent out – new mast and rigging plus extras such as a proper heater. And I doubt if we could have managed it without the sterling efforts of our trustees back in the UK, especially ex-OSTAR skipper Chris Smith, not to mention the RAF who freighted out the new mast and rigging which just fitted into the hold of a TriStar. Their charge was almost equal to the price of the gear itself but, honourably, the insurers eventually paid out.

Dodo was ready and it was decision time. Which way to go? Cape Horn direct or chicken out and head through the Magellan Straits and Beagle Channel? Or, as we'd originally intended, sail back to Antarctica and then on round Cape Horn? Perhaps it was too late in the year for that…

Fortunately we had experienced and expert brains to pick. Acknowledged gurus of Antarctic sailing, Jerome and Sally Poncet, arrived in *Damien 2* (back from South Georgia), and Philippe and Christine Poupon, resting from the break-up of Philippe's racing machine *Fleury Michon*, turned up in their cruising yacht. Jerome assured me that the Antarctic would be open well into April – and some years even into May – and also that April could be a good month to round the Horn, 'More gales; less severe,' was how he put it.

I finally decided to go down to Antarctica. The crew were a little apprehensive, but they seemed to accept my choice. I had known them throughout their school years, they had sailed with me before on my boat and I had become accustomed to making the decisions, although in hindsight perhaps without as much consultation as there might have been. On the whole we all got on very well, but while I was under pressure with *Dodo*'s repairs and insurance issues, life on board did have its tensions. One evening at supper, for example, Henchy could not resist goading me about something – I cannot remember what – until, exasperated, I picked up my plate of spaghetti and threw it at him. The crew all rushed off to the watering hole they had discovered in Stanley, leaving me alone on the boat.

While the morning cup of tea I took to Henchy as a peace offering restored good relations, all attempts to cure our recalcitrant HF radio came to nought. Stanley's resident expert tried everything, but we never did manage to get it to transmit properly. It was at this stage, too, that Howesy, wise man, decided that enough was enough, left us and flew back to the UK.

So, at noon on Thursday 17 March we slipped our lines from the Town Pier and sailed out into the Drake Passage again with a new mast and, dangling from our stern gantry, half a sheep from Jerome – no need for a freezer here. New rig or not, the light breeze made for frustratingly slow progress. The crew countered boredom by listening to the England v Wales rugby match, which seemed somewhat incongruous as we were sailing in what can be the world's most fearful sea. Condensation was a persistent problem and, mile on mile, it was growing colder. We did have a decent cabin heater now although the crew accused me, falsely of course, of not allowing them to light it as much as they would have liked. With some use of the engine towards the end, the crossing took seven days and five hours, only one hour less than it had under jury rig.

Sailing back into Antarctica through English Strait more than made up for the dull Drake Passage. The wind blew hard and we tacked inside the Asses Ears' rocks to save time and distance. Numerous swirls in the water had us wondering whether all the rocks in the water were marked on the Admiralty chart. But the hydrographers and surveyors had been meticulous and those violent swirls and eddies were caused not by submerged rocks but by the tide. One of the larger rocks turned out to be a whale blowing to starboard. With a huge swell from astern and wind and tide from ahead – we were moving at 6 knots through the water but only 2 over the ground – we swept sedately through the narrows past the headland of Fort William.

We had, of course, been in these waters not long before and I could not resist revisiting the naval base, Arturo Prat. And there, set in concrete and complete with signs to Valparaiso, Base Marsh and so on, stood the top half of our old mast inscribed with the words, 'Trozo del mastil de *Dodo's Delight* 1994.' 'You,' the locals told us, 'are part of the history of Arturo Prat now.' I think they meant it kindly. They topped up our water and diesel (we could have run the engine more after all) then led us into their glacial pool via the submerged rock we had encountered the previous time of course – and entertained us far into the night in fine Chilean style.

Despite the late night we managed to make an early start towards Deception Island. It was not long before we were fighting our way through a fierce blizzard – a first for all of us, and on went the ski goggles. I had never before seen snow stick so fully to the sails or seen the decks so white.

Neptune's Bellows is the aptly named cleft which forms the entrance to the huge volcanic crater which is Deception Island – and with a big following sea building, it did not look particularly inviting.

Above *Dodo's Delight* through the iceberg, Sortehul, Upernavik, Greenland. Photo: Bob Shepton Collection

Below This beautiful land: Upernavik, Greenland. Photo: Nico Favresse

Above Preparing to winter alone in Greenland, 2004–2005. Photo: Bob Shepton Collection

Below A leopard seal after its breakfast of penguin, Gerlache Strait, Antarctica. Photo: Bob Shepton Collection

Above Anchored in Stella Creek, by the BAS Faraday Base as it was, Antarctica, 1994.
Photo: Bob Shepton Collection

Below Cape Horn can be rough. Photo: Bob Shepton Collection

Opposite *Dodo's Delight* surveys the big north wall of *Sandersons Hope*, Upernavik, climbed in 2000.
Photo: Graham Austick

Above *Dodo's Delight* caught in pack ice, Bylot Island, Canada, 2001. Photo: Polly Murray

Below Overnight camp on glacier, halfway on Bylot Island traverse. Photo: Bob Shepton Collection

Above Walrus and *Billy Budd*, Bethune Inlet, Devon Island, arctic Canada, 2006. Photo: Clive Shute

Below Author on rifle practice, in case of polar bears. Photo: Clive Shute

Above Starting the first ascent of Pt 900, Northumberland Island, far north Greenland, 2009.
Photo: 'Martin'

Below Stopping for a tea break on the way down. Photo: 'Martin'

Above Winter came early to Aasiaat, Greenland in 2009. Photo: Thomas Gough

Below An iceberg showing differing sea levels each time a chunk falls off. Photo: Bob Shepton Collection

Above Landing climbers by dinghy for Brown Balls climb on Intermediate Wall, 2010. Photo: Nico Favresse

Below The Wild Bunch playing Tarzan swings while the boat was grounded. Photo: Nico Favresse

Above 'The Devil's Brew' – a 'kind' gift to the author from the Wild Bunch! They then named their climb on *Impossible Wall* after it. Photo: Sean Villaneuva

Opposite Climbing the first pitch of Devil's Brew, *Impossible Wall*, in 2010. Photo: Bob Shepton Collection

Opposite Above the clouds, *Impossible Wall*. Photo: Sean Villaneuva

Below Portaledges were used for sleep and cooking, and music! Photo: Nico Favresse

Bottom The Wild Bunch having just topped out of Devil's Brew, *Impossible Wall*. Photo: Sean Villaneuva

Above The author seeking refreshment on Never Again! Photo: Nico Favresse

Below Sean takes a bath in mid-Atlantic. Photo: Sean Villaneuva

Above A curious South African custom, or a way of acclimatising quickly? Photo: Bob Shepton Collection

Below Resting on a portaledge on *Impossible Wall*, 2012. Photo: Steve Bradshaw

Above Anchored in 2012 by the three graves from Franklin's ill-fated expedition in 1845, Beechey Island, Northwest Passage.
Photo: Bob Shepton Collection

Left The author with his Yachtsman of the Year 2013 trophy, January 2014.
Photo: Bob Shepton Collection

In broken water, with spray shooting up the cliffs to starboard we ran through cautiously under a small headsail alone, careful to keep to starboard so we were well away from the underwater shelf marked on the chart to port. Safely through, we turned sharp to starboard and went up to the far end of Whalers Bay to anchor in volcanic sand close inshore. This was one of those anchorages where you put your hook down in 3 metres of water and by the time you have paid out the chain you are floating in 20 metres. Despite the stiff breeze, the anchor held firm through the night.

In the morning we explored the British base and whaling station, abandoned after the volcanic eruption of 1969. The living quarters had been filled with coke cinders. There we found newspapers dating back to the 1930s and, strangely, left behind in one of the hangers was a fully intact and serviceable piston-engine plane which, I was told, had never been flown. Incidentally, it was here that I, knowing that their bite can be quite serious, discovered I could run faster and farther than a fur seal which had taken offence at my presence.

Later that day we moved on to an impressive anchorage in the north-west corner of Deception Island. Telefon Bay is a small, round, sea-filled crater – also formed during the 1969 eruption – and getting over the shallow sill into the little bay certainly concentrated the mind. We rowed ashore and climbed the snow-covered hills by the anchorage for a bird's-eye view of this desolate, dramatic landscape.

We woke the following morning to find the temperature had dropped to minus 10°C. The anemometer atop the mast had frozen solid in the blizzard, and frozen it looked set to remain. We motored out under a blue sky and sunshine; in spite of continuous high pressure this turned out to be one of relatively few clear and sunny days we would see during our time in Antarctica.

What little sailing we were able to do took us to the east of Trinity Island – far from ideal because ice collects to leeward of objects and islands. Having said that, motoring through bands of brash ice for the first time and past icebergs big and small on that clear, moonlit night was an unforgettable experience. But it was tiring on the helm and eventually I wanted sleep. On the north shore of Chionos Island, just off Trinity Island, we found a rather open anchorage in an inlet by a penguin rookery and took to our bunks.

In the half-light of dawn we watched the penguins form orderly queues along the rocky shore. In quick succession they dived in and swam alongside us on the surface, past both sides of the boat – off on a fishing expedition, we presumed. Suddenly, a large iceberg off our stern became detached from the seabed on the spring tide and started drifting towards the boat. Just as it seemed about to hit us the current steered it away, but not so very far away. It was time to fetch our anchor.

Throughout the previous night I had been aware of rumbling and crashing noises somewhere to starboard. Now, as we motored along under Trinity Island's spectacular ice cliffs, the source of the noise became obvious. The cliffs are, in fact, the foot of a big glacier – as we realised when a huge block of ice fell into the sea as we passed. To my relief the sea and floating ice chunks quietened the tidal wave quite quickly so that *Dodo's Delight* merely rocked up and down a bit when the swell reached us.

We chugged along uneventfully through ice brought up from the south on the prevailing wind until we reached the Gerlache Strait. Here, off Cape Herschel, we encountered an extensive field of bergs, brash and bergy bits. We focused hard, searching out leads and threading our way through with care. Our only digression was to circle an ice floe to take a closer look at a basking leopard seal. Patches of blood on the ice around him were all that remained of his penguin breakfast. The power, majesty and sheer size of Antarctica engenders a sense of the primordial – the antithesis of and far from the Mediterranean's madding crowds. Once, we thought we saw a Japanese fishing boat in the far distance but that was it; we saw no other vessels in all our time in the region.

There was a much bigger and even denser field of bergy bits to contend with off Hughes Bay. Dood, up the mast on a spreader on the look-out for leads (stretches of open water through the ice), saw it first and shouted – there, in a lead, was a huge, nuclear submarine of a humpback whale swimming straight for the boat. It dived just short of us. It all happened so fast that there was nothing we could have done about it – such a close call left us pretty shocked, but only afterwards.

This late in the year, darkness was beginning to creep into the Antarctic night so while there was still light we made way towards Murray Harbour and an anchorage recommended by Jerome Poncet. We found, however, that ice and snow had covered the island and inlet, so instead we motored into the main harbour, its entrance marked by a huge, grounded berg. Murray Harbour is a circular, rocky amphitheatre and ridiculously deep. The echo sounder had been giving us trouble so we could not be sure if it was reading true. There might have been shallower water to anchor in closer to the shore, but without a trustworthy echo sounder it was too risky to try.

We did finally find a shallow inlet just inside the entrance to port. Because the anchor was only lying on a rocky shelf we rigged fore and aft mooring lines as well: on one side of the inlet we banged pitons into rocks – near some seals who, this time, did not try to chase me – while into the snow on the opposite bank we hammered stakes cut from old angle iron we had found in Port Stanley's rubbish dump. With the uncertain lie of the anchor a night watch was a given. In fact, the anchor supported by the lines stayed put but, curiously, during the night most of the ice in the harbour took off on the spring tide and was carried out to sea. The boat was not in the main line of fire, but we did have to fend off quite a few passing chunks.

In the morning we climbed the low hill above the anchorage and took pictures. But we soon had the engine running for the comparatively short hop to Foyn Harbour, as that day's mission was to locate the wreck of an old whaler. A meander through a series of inter-connecting fjords brought us to the wreck, lying slightly on its side and with its stern half submerged. Over time, wind, sea and ice will doubtless see it off, but tied up alongside we deemed the old ship to be our best and safest stopping place so far in Antarctica.

Our next excursion took us by dinghy to a nearby island where a collection of old wooden whaling dories was drawn up on the snow. Although these were not light, open boats but rather heavily planked and decked all over, we were reminded of the dories depicted in Rudyard Kipling's *Captains Courageous* and Herman Melville's *Moby Dick*. There appeared to be no fittings for mast or oars which left us wondering how they were propelled. An ice cave in the glacial cliff by our mooring provided another photo opportunity – not least because the meltwater streaming off its roof had formed one perfect, small stalagmite and an equally perfect stalactite. I thought I had better warn Pebs, who stayed in the cave while I fetched my camera, that cliffs such as these are always, very slowly, moving and it was only a matter of time before this ice cave collapsed.

That night, safely alongside the wreck and with no ice in the bay, we slept long and deep. Next day, our water supply replenished with pure, delicious meltwater, we had enough wind to warrant hoisting our sails. Dodging ice, we tacked down the Gerlache Strait then, after a night in a rather insecure anchorage by Lion Island, we sailed – with five killer whales in our wake – down the Neumayer Channel. The whales looked strangely benign when they rose out of the water, grinning superciliously as if they were simply showing off. There are, of course, grim accounts of boats being rammed by killer whales, but the five we met gave us no trouble, and after a while they lost all interest in the boat and swam off.

There was a huge volume of ice floating in the Neumayer Channel, especially in its dog leg, but the sun shone and the mountains glittered. A thick mist hung over our intended destination, Port Lockroy, while Dorian Bay was bathed in sunlight: we decided to stay in the sun. The entrance was narrow and shallow and making it through and over its rocky sill put our pilotage skills to the test.

Sunday, we decided, should be a day of rest. Ashore, the huts used respectively by the British and Argentineans stood empty. How, I wondered, had things gone between huts and crews at the time of the 1982 conflict? I climbed the nearby snow slopes to look across to the now mist-free, well-protected small base of Port Lockroy, unmanned at this time of year. The crew meantime had headed off to a penguin colony. They returned ecstatic; they had been able to get quite close and had quietly watched the penguins at work and play for quite some time. It had been a fine highlight to a great day: sunshine, tremendous vistas of snow-covered mountains and now another peaceful night aboard with no anchor watch, although I did notice some reefs astern uncovered by the tide in the night.

Next day as we approached the Lemaire Channel we chanced upon two humpback whales sleeping on the surface. Disturbed, they woke up and dived, with those characteristic tail flukes the last to disappear, splashless, like perfect high divers. The channel was certainly impressive, with mountains on either side which have only recently been climbed. As always, routes up them beckoned but we were not in climbing mode on this trip and had brought no gear.

There was plenty of ice on the approach and down the channel's length. A big iceberg was grounded at the far end in the middle of the narrowest part of the channel. We chose to pass on the starboard side and just squeezed between the iceberg and the sheer cliff, taking pictures as we went. Once through, the motionless statues of ice standing in the utter silence and stillness, in dead calm water, could not fail to make a deep impression on young and old alike.

The anchorage at Peterman Island, which we had considered a possibility, looked to be filled with small bergs, so we tried radioing the British Faraday base, as it was then, on the off chance that they might be able to advise. 'Faraday Base, Faraday Base, this is *Dodo's Delight, Dodo's Delight,* do you read? Over.' I was amazed when they came straight back sounding rather urgent. Later they told us that the Chileans at Arturo Prat had been worried. It had never occurred to us that anybody would have been worrying about us as we made our unhurried way south. They also told us that if we had not called within the next day or two a rescue operation would have been mounted. We found this all rather surprising.

Faraday also gave us advice as to what they considered would be the best approach, but we missed their recommendation – the 'French Channel' as they called it – in the confusion of ice and snowy islands, and so pressed on down the Penola Channel instead. This led us to the Meek Channel which was choc-a-block with brash ice with no leads at all. Reluctant to go back, we started to motor through as gently as possible with Henchy and Pebs using the genoa and jib poles to push the bigger blocks away. Thus we were able to make our way gingerly through to the base. Down below, the sound of the ice scraping along the hull had been terrible: I was convinced it must be scouring the hull badly, but when thousands of miles later we had the boat lifted out there was not a scratch on her. Clearly glassfibre is stronger than we think.

Some of the base personnel were standing on the quayside at Faraday as we motored in looking for a spot to come alongside, but they waved us on and round the corner into another channel. We followed their directions, breaking through thin sea ice into Stella Creek where we dropped the anchor. The boat was not going anywhere that night.

For some reason Mohican haircuts seemed to predominate among the young scientists of Faraday, but they made us most welcome and helped us as much as they were allowed, and perhaps a little more besides. We replenished stores and they even allowed us to top up our tank with diesel when the base commander was not looking. That evening they invited us to drinks. I got talking to one Arkwright, a skilled joiner, and was surprised when he said, 'I won't be working on Monday of course'. 'Oh, why not?' I asked. 'Well, you know it's Easter weekend?' I had clean forgotten; you lose all account of days and weeks at sea but, for a man of the cloth, that was no excuse.

Another night they had us to supper and presented us with a rather fine plaque with the Faraday Base emblem on it, which we later screwed onto the main cabin bulkhead. We gave them a bottle of whisky as a token gesture, but as their bar was more than well stocked I realised by their muted thanks that this was really 'coals to Newcastle'. Their radio man was most concerned at our lack of long-range communication for the voyage north and went to great trouble to fit one of their small HF transceivers. This involved emptying the entire contents of the cockpit locker of gear accumulated over the years. But eventually the radio was fitted and the gear stowed back more or less as before. Alas, the radio worked for two nights and then we lost contact altogether. But it was kindly meant.

Three or four days after our arrival we found ourselves once again pushing out through brash ice into the Drake Passage. Mainly so I could say we had got a little farther south than my friend Willy Ker on his Antarctic voyage two years previously, we went down to 65° 15.32S. High latitude cruising is of course entirely non-competitive… In fact, I rather wish we had gone farther south still, as during the night the sea looked clear on the radar, but I thought we had better play safe. After all, ahead of us to the north-west lay Cape Horn, towards which we set our bow, bound for the Pacific and Easter Island.

Dodo's Delight continued via Cape Horn to reach Easter Island on the night of 8/9 May, a passage of 3788 miles from Antarctica round the Horn in thirty-four days.

ANGELS TO THE RESCUE

If you can meet with Triumph and Disaster,
And treat those two imposters just the same …
IF, RUDYARD KIPLING

If you are determined to do mad things then you must have a good – I am tempted to say mad – crew, and Keith, Nigel, Emily and Phil were surely slightly crazy to agree to sail with me to Greenland. Keith was a former chief instructor and the hard man of the Scottish National Outdoor Centre's Glenmore Lodge, where he had worked for more than twenty years. I nicknamed him Gimlet for the way he set his face like flint and bored straight on towards his objective. Nigel and Emily were partners and both were enthusiastic climbers and skiers; they were also keen sailors and had left their boat on my mooring at Appin in Scotland when we departed for Greenland. Phil lived in Kendal where he had been manager of The North Face shop; he was a keen fell runner and he sailed his own boat, a Contessa 26. In short, between them the crew held a number of mountaineering and/or ski instructor qualifications, and all bar Gimlet, who opted to fly out to Greenland and join us in Nuuk, were experienced sailors.

The North Atlantic, the 'meanest Atlantic crossing of them all', lived up to its billing as a deep depression established itself in the mid-Atlantic, south of Iceland. Long tentacles of isobars stretched across from Greenland all the way to Scotland. We crawled across the face of the chart and passed right through the eye of the depression. Here the wind, which hitherto had been from the south-west, died completely leaving us in a very confused sea, and then some hours later slammed in from the north. We had been aiming to keep well south of Cape Farewell, that cape of storms, but were soon forced to choose between tacking up towards the cape or Newfoundland. We chose the former, but after zigzagging against strong north-westerlies (by now), and making little progress, eventually doused the jib and hove-to under trysail alone.

Motor sailing later against another strong north-west wind round the aptly named Cape Desolation, the crew were awestruck by the large icebergs we passed in the cloudy dusk. In total, apart from one day of calm and sunshine in the Davis Strait and half a day's beam reaching in the Atlantic which brought everyone up on deck, it had been eighteen days of hard slogging against the wind, all the way, some 2000 miles from Appin to Nuuk.

Gimlet, with a confused account of sleeping in a tent and then on a bench in a bus shelter, eventually found us there. After refuelling we continued northwards up the coast, still against the wind, until we closed the 15-mile long Kangerdluarssuqssuaq Fjord, keeping to the line of soundings depicted on the chart which, at one point, dipped scarily down to just 2 metres below the keel. On the huge silt bank at the far end of the fjord we dropped anchor as we had done four years earlier.

From this anchorage at the head of Kangerdluarssuqssuaq we made a number of first ascents: Nigel and Emily of a worthy, well-defined peak on the south side of the fjord ending in a snow ridge and dome, while Gimlet, Phil and I took in a less well-defined peak with a lot of loose rock on the north side, but which had not been climbed before.

We made another hard and frustrating climb. The peak, marked as 560 metres on the Saga maps, looked promising and impressive, and we set off with high hopes, Gimlet striding ahead. It was a long slog, much of it up horribly loose scree and rock. Some way up I came upon a new navigational aid, left behind by the ex-Glenmore Lodge chief instructor – an arrow drawn in the snow pointing onward with BOB in large letters by it. The final approach was up a long snow slope. It was late evening and I plodded on in a state of near exhaustion to find Gimlet waiting for me near the top, in order that I should be first on top, which was kind. And at the top there was… a huge and well-constructed cairn. We were not the first after all. What a let-down, after all that effort.

The descent took almost as long. With such an age difference, Gimlet strode on, but towards the end I found him waiting under a rock making a brew, after which he packed up the stove and continued on his way. It was a welcome gesture. Although the brew had helped I was in a bad way by this stage (the downside of getting old) and chose to settle down under the shelter of the rock (it was raining now) and get some sleep. A couple of hours later I rolled up my karrimat and sleeping bag and walked the final 8 kilometres down the river valley to the boat, where I arrived worn out. Later Gimlet said it was the hardest mountain day he had ever experienced, and the state of his feet, which he proudly displayed, proved his point.

Akuliarusinguaq

We then moved north via Sisimiut, Aasiaat, the scenic Vaigat Channel and so to Ingia Fjord at the far northern end of Uummannaq Fjord. On route we passed over or near rocks off Ubekendt Island marked slightly alarmingly on the chart as PA (position approximate). I had been to this tongue-twisting region before. Even when it is possible to spell these names, and that seems to vary, it is almost impossible to pronounce them correctly. We again found ourselves in serious ground with loose rock, large unconsolidated boulder fields, glaciers, moraines and well-defined mountains. We made a number of first ascents where sometimes the difficulties were caused by the nature of the terrain rather than anything technical. To reach one ridge with four unclimbed summits along its length, Phil and I had to clamber up about 300 metres (1000 feet) of loose rock and scree; one step forwards and two backwards, or so it seemed.

One particularly notable ascent, or lack of it, springs to mind: a peak marked 2000 metres on the map, some distance inland. Now 2000 metres is a magic number; these peaks are the highest on the west coast of Greenland and I persuaded Gimlet that we should do it. It involved traversing big boulder fields, passing under a hanging glacier, scrambling up boulders in a gully at the side of the glacier, and then a long ascent along the top of a lateral moraine before moving across to traverse up the glacier itself.

Some way up we made a gear dump so as to make a quick first ascent of a subsidiary peak to the side, and struggled on over loose rock, Gimlet out in front as usual. A while later he passed me coming down while I was still struggling up. When we finally met up again down on the glacier I was shattered, and all for leaving the gear and returning for an ascent in a day or two, going back to the boat now.

Instead, Gimlet suggested bivvying for a few hours and tackling the main (we'd only done a subsidiary!) peak there and then. I reckoned I would never make it. Picking up his gear, Gimlet stomped down ahead and was asleep in his bunk by the time I got back.

Next morning there was no way I could persuade Gimlet, or any of the others, to go up again. But I had left my sleeping bag and gear up there and was certainly not going to abandon it all. An interesting difference in attitude was becoming apparent. Whereas I had a burning ambition to climb mountains no one had ever climbed before, Gimlet seemed more interested in enjoying a pleasant mountain day. 'You lack the killer instinct,' I said trying to goad him into action, to no avail. So I had to set off on my own the next day.

Over the boulder fields, under the hanging glacier, up the gully I trudged, across the lateral moraine and over the glacier to where I had left my gear. I ate a sandwich; there was still a long way to go. What looked an easy snow slope from a distance now nearly killed me; with every step my feet sank deep into soft snow. I began to wonder whether I was going to make it. A steeper rock-strewn bluff beyond gave some relief, and then a final steep snow slope led at last to the rounded summit, which by the not too accurate altimeter on my watch I made to be 2060 metres. It was about midnight by now but still light. I rather pointedly named the mountain *Solo* Snow Dome, and felt relieved and elated that I had conquered it – though you never really conquer a mountain. But at least it had not conquered me.

A little way down I radioed back to tell of my triumph. I expect I woke them up, but they did answer and told me they had left a tent for me at the bottom. Early that morning I stumbled upon it and crashed into it, exhausted. Later Gimlet came over in the dinghy, with some difficulty owing to the ice, which was only justice, and rescued me.

Next day we crossed to the other side of the fjord to do some more climbing. I had anchored close to the gravel beach to make landing the climbers easier, and was now alone on the boat. Suddenly a huge swell picked *Dodo* up and threw her on to the beach on her beam ends, grinding her keel into the gravel. Luckily the engine started first time. I waited for the next wave to ride high up the beach, gunned the engine hard, and we slid off into deeper water. Only then did I have time to be frightened. Icebergs shed sections from time to time, explode or roll right over, but these have had little effect on the boat in the past. On this occasion, however, a massive berg must have calved from the Umiamako Isbrae, the huge glacier some 10 or 11 kilometres to the east, and a tidal wave had then made its way silently, inexorably down the fjord.

The following morning we headed down the channel on the east side of the big island of Qeqertarssuaq to the settlement of Nugaatsiaq at the southern end of the island. This channel is normally ice strewn and difficult, but was quite friendly this time. It so happened that the oil supply vessel came into the harbour while we were there to top up their supplies for the winter, and Nigel and Em managed in the indomitable manner of the young to hitch a lift south. I cannot imagine it happening in over-regulated Europe, but it saved them the hefty airfare from Upernavik later.

Meanwhile Gimlet, Phil and I headed north again, stopping at Upernavik Kujalleq (formerly Sondre Upernavik) to take on fuel. It must have been half-term or an extended lunch break, for all the local school children, or so it seemed, came down to the boat. I have a photo of *Dodo* crammed to the gunwales, with poor Phil trying to breathe amid the press of small bodies. 'What is your name?' asked one of the children; obviously the first phrase they learn in English.

On the beach nearby a woman stood alone flensing a seal with a sharp knife in the ancient way. Not a thing is wasted, the meat is for eating, the blubber for fat and oil, the skin for clothing – and it is still better than modern fibres. Two dead seals lay underwater by the jetty, waiting their turn. Greenland is a fabulous juxtaposition of the old and the new.

Upernavik and the Far North

Having decided that he was more of a climber than a sailor, Gimlet opted to fly home from Upernavik. And now Phil, under pressure from home, felt he had no option but to return, despite being embarrassed that he might be letting me down for the next rather serious leg of the expedition. Thus Gimlet and Phil departed and, after some delay with the flights in Ilulissat, Polly, Tash (or Tashy) and Jess (or Jessy) arrived. 'Bob's Angels' as the trio dubbed themselves, and which I have always taken as a tremendous compliment, stood on the quay, smiling and looking 'angelic'.

They were good-looking young ladies, and two of them at least were also as tough as nails. Polly was the first Scots girl to climb Everest, unguided and in a private expedition, and she and Tashy had climbed Mt McKinley in Alaska and skied all the way down on their telemark skis. Both were qualified ski instructors and had instructed in Chamonix for a number of years. I also had the pleasure of marrying Polly to Richard Haworth (of High Latitudes yachting) on a hillside near their home on the east side of Scotland some years later. Jessy, perhaps not quite so steely but still quietly determined, has now for a number of years skippered a charter boat out in the Caribbean.

Our aim was to go to the far north to visit the town of Qaanaq, and the small Inuit settlement of Siorapaluk which is the northernmost indigenous community in the world[*], and then the long-abandoned erstwhile most northerly Inuit settlement of Etah in Smith Sound. The girls would be climbing and making a film and, if possible, we hoped to sail farther north in Greenland than any glassfibre production boat had been before.

One night off Cape York, Tashy woke me; I was wanted on deck. The radar looked as if it had caught a bad dose of the measles. We were surrounded by a huge field of icebergs that presumably had calved off the several glaciers to the north of us. Having just woken

---

[*] Longyearbear in Svalbard is farther north, but the population is not indigenous.

up it took me a moment to take stock, but Tashy, though not unduly worried, had done the correct thing of waking the skipper in such circumstances. The nights were darker now, but we could still see enough to weave our way between the bergs, bergy bits and growlers, albeit rather unwisely still under sail. We met more bergs farther on, off the Pituffik glacier, but by then it was in full daylight and avoiding them was a little easier.

Qaanaq is an open roadstead with no protection; it is not a good anchorage. The Royal Cruising Club's pilot book used to recommend anchoring off the reef guarding the settlement to keep clear of iceberg alley, but what it did not say was that then puts you slap bang in the bergy bits and growler alley. Once, at anchor and while the crew were ashore, I was forced to fire up the engine to try to avoid a small berg which must have weighed several tons. The ploy failed and the berg stuck fast against the boat still anchored, threatening to tear away stanchions and rigging. I tried to pole it away, but it was no good and in the end I had to give up. Distraught, I dashed back to the cockpit and turned off the engine. Then the berg broke itself free of the boat, but at the same moment the bow rode up on a growler, 'Lucky Westerlys built strong boats,' I thought as we slid back down again. That evening three local carpenters – two Danes and one Inuit – rowed out to visit armed with a crate of Tuborg. We sat on deck, chatting in the sun and, although they were naturally more interested in talking to the ladies of the crew than to me, they offered us all showers and hospitality next day in their homes.

Strong winds kept us on our toes one night at anchor in McCormick Fjord. We stopped here because the crew were reading *My Arctic Journal*, Josephine Peary's account of the winter she spent there with her husband, Robert Peary. The girls were thrilled when they found the site, close to the shoreline, of the winter quarters the couple had shared until Robert set out that spring on one of his attempts on the North Pole. And we also called in at Siorapaluk, or Siorapalup as it is in Inuit, a small village or settlement with the usual numbers of lively children around, and a flensed seal skin drying on a rack by a traditional kayak.

From Siorapaluk we continued north and round Cape Alexander, mainland Greenland's most westerly extremity, and on towards Etah. I shall not forget that day in a hurry. We avoided the icebergs close to the northern shore which appeared to be blocking the entrance to the fjord, but as we passed the island promontory to the south we were hit by huge katabatic winds blasting down the fjord from the glacier to the east of Etah. As we approached the village some rocks on the scree slope above seemed to be moving, but the rocks turned out to be a herd of musk oxen probably disturbed by the sound of our engine. The wind was hammering relentlessly down the fjord and every time we put down the anchor it dragged through the soft mud. At last, and by now it was practically on the beach, we managed to dig it in hard enough to let the girls dinghy ashore and inspect the remains of the settlement.

The crew were fascinated by what they found. Three or four of the old dwellings were still partly standing. The houses again had turf roofs and walls of turf interspersed with a layer of stones, some still had their original stoves and beds and inside one stood a pair of boots as if waiting for the owner to slip his feet back into them. In the past several famous explorers had spent time here, including Robert Peary, Knud Rasmussen, Donald MacMillan and Lord Edward Shackleton, Ernest Shackleton's youngest son.

The girls were on their way back in the dinghy when a huge gust plucked the anchor off the shore: they had to row strong and hard to catch the boat before the furious wind drove *Dodo* out of reach. Wind and sea thwarted all attempts to go farther north so we slipped back to a safe anchorage on a silt bank between Cape Alexander and Sutherland Island to rest up and wait for the weather to moderate. As soon as conditions allowed we would cross Smith Sound towards Cape Isabella on Ellesmere Island.

This expedition, though private, was part-funded by the Scottish Mountaineering Trust whose terms require expeditions to undertake a scientific project in addition to the climbing element. To fulfil that brief we proposed to measure the salinity versus fresh water content of the water in Smith Sound, which in turn would indicate how much and how fast the ice in the Arctic Ocean is melting. Martin Doble, who was working at the Scottish Association for Marine Science (SAMS) at Dunstaffnage and lived near my home, had acquired us a Conductivity Temperature Depth (CTD) recorder and now that the wind was dropping its time had come.

The plan was to motor across the sound lowering the CTD's probe to 400 metres every 6 kilometres or so. The first cast of the line went out at an angle so I attached diving weights to the probe's bottom and at the next attempt it went down more or less vertically. However, I had not anticipated how much effort it would take to retrieve the weighted line from such a great depth; I had not conceived how long 400 metres of line really was in practice. Even with the line looped around a winch to help give some purchase it was heavy going and we had to repeat the haul five or six times. But I had Amazonian women aboard. The last three casts were made within old, heavy pack ice, but it was open and now the sea was calm and the sun was shining. 'This is divine,' said Polly. A gift from God, indeed – blue sky, sun, sparkling white pack ice (albeit with the odd polar bear prints), calm deep water and the snow-covered mountains on Ellesmere Island ahead.

Out of the pack ice and back in open water we turned north; we wanted to find out how far up Smith Sound we could push. Remote from civilisation, it was still and silent; seals and narwhal swam nearby. Frazil ice started to appear, then floating 'pancakes' in the sea, growing ever larger and converging as we crept farther north. Then, overcome by the whole scene, the 'angel' on watch carved straight through a 'dinner plate' the size of a dining table and at 78° 32'N, near Cache Point, I gave the order to turn round. Exciting, yes, but I had no intention of spending the winter here. *Dodo*'s hull made a clear, visible loop in the icy mush as we made our escape.

After a brief debate about whether to head for Refuge Harbour for the night we pressed on through more frazil ice in gathering darkness and increasing wind, and into the comparatively ice-free polynya of these parts, and so round Cape Alexander to our snug anchorage on the incongruous sand bar inside Sutherland Island.

We had, so far as I was aware, sailed farther north in Greenland than any other glassfibre production yacht on either side (although I have since found out that *Vagabond'eur*, a 40-foot Beneteau, sailed seven miles farther in 1988), which seemed a fitting achievement for *Dodo's Delight,* now in her twenty-fifth year.

But it was as well we had aborted when we did; we were stormbound for three days – the decks disappeared completely under snow. Restless one evening the crew jumped ship, landed on the steep side of Sutherland Island and climbed to the top, for something to do. We made one further attempt to leave the island, but quickly returned.

When we did eventually make it south, it was to anchor again in McCormick Fjord in preparation for Polly and Tashy's ski traverse of Herbert Island the next day. This had not been done before, and it was going to be a tough challenge. But these angels were tough cookies.

It was a beautiful morning with the snow on the island painted pink in the dawn light, but I felt anxious entering water by Herbert Island marked *urent* (foul) on the chart. The rocks below were visible and, with Jessy keeping a watch ahead and me with an eye on the echo sounder, we motored gingerly towards the shore. We put down an anchor and Jessy dinghied Polly and Tash over to the island.

Jessy and I then took the boat round to the island's west side to wait in rather rolly and not very well protected anchorages for the skiers to return. The traverse would take perhaps three days, so we had plenty of time to talk, 'You know Jess,' I said, 'I cannot understand how you can be so artistic and admiring of the beauty around you and yet not believe in a Creator.' Jessy was having none of it!

It was during our long wait for Polly and Tashy that I fully realised why my wife Kate had sometimes been worried when I was late back from climbing, or some other risky activity. It is always worse for those left behind. By late afternoon on the third day I was beginning to worry about them despite Jessy's assurances that they would be fine. Sure enough, later that evening they radioed in to say they were on their way down. That night, while the three women slept I watched a huge, heaving, breathing iceberg drift dangerously close to the boat. But it passed and we got away with it.

The following day we returned to Qaanaq without drama and feeling good about Polly and Tashy's achievement, which was indeed considerable. They had started by clambering up 760 metres (2500 feet) carrying their skis, tent, food, fuel and equipment, to reach the ridge. It then took them three days to traverse the 30 kilometres along the top of the ridge, sometimes skiing, sometimes scrambling up rocky pitches with skis on their backs, and sometimes enduring strong winds camping at night. The British explorer Wally Herbert (the names were coincidental) had spent a winter with his family in the village below some years earlier, but the actual traverse had never been done before.

Dodo had one more scare on the return to Upernavik. After putting in to Barden Bugt to catch some sleep we were hit next morning by winds of Force 8 gusting to more than 40 knots. We dropped all sail, turned on the engine and clawed our way back to what we hoped would be a viable anchorage behind a glacial moraine, although it was not until we had laid out two anchors and put a weight down the chain of one of them that we felt at all secure.

From then on, while the longer, darker nights did make pilotage more difficult when we were in the vicinity of ice, the passage went without incident and we made it to Upernavik on 1 October. The 'angels' headed for the airport and home. I made ready to winter alone in the ice.

After the triumphs we had enjoyed, *Dodo* and I were to meet disaster. It had little to do with the conditions, or the cold; a mistake of my own making, it is told in the prologue.

05

MOUNTAINS AND MEN (AND WOMEN)

Whatever you can do, or dream you can, begin it,
Boldness has genius, power and magic in it.

WRONGLY ATTRIBUTED TO JOHANN WOLFGANG VON GOETHE IN
W.H. MURRAY, *THE SCOTTISH HIMALAYAN EXPEDITION*

From 1995, I had begun to combine sailing with climbing. The east coast of Greenland has received a lot of attention from climbers; the west coast by contrast has been neglected. In a sailing boat it is touch and go whether you can approach the east coast because of the *storis*, the Arctic ice brought down on the east Greenland current, whereas you are pretty well guaranteed to get into wherever you like on the west coast. And that is where we were headed, the challenge to emulate the feats of one of the climbing world's heroes.

THE ARCTIC, LIKE TILMAN? WHY NOT?

Well known for his climbing feats in the Himalayas before and after the Second World War, Bill Tilman, one of the few people who fought in both world conflicts, had won a Military Cross and Bar, and Distinguished Service Order. In his latter years he bought an old Bristol Channel pilot cutter, *Mischief*, in order to sail to remote regions and climb mountains. Why not follow his example? Antarctica was a long way away, but one could get to the Arctic and back in one summer. So started a decade-long series of Tilman-type expeditions, sailing across the North Atlantic and climbing mountains from the boat in Greenland and Arctic Canada.

The crossing from Scotland to Greenland is known for its usual big winds and rough seas – depressions swing up from Newfoundland towards Iceland and the Faroes so you nearly always get clobbered by one or two gales, far out in the middle of the Atlantic. I have come to call it 'gale alley', although every year is different. In 1998, in a storm off Cape Farewell, we had been knocked down and sustained some damage. By contrast the year 2000 was different, with a huge high pressure area of 1040mb forming and spreading from Scotland across the Atlantic to Greenland. For hundreds of miles we had virtually no wind. We were forced to motor for long periods, but a 33-foot sailing boat cannot carry unlimited fuel. We tried running the engine at slow revs to eke out the diesel, and this at least gave us the satisfaction of moving, although progress was slow. Would the fuel last? Eventually the high moved and conditions reverted to something like normal. For three or four days strong head winds made the going uncomfortable, but we were moving. Furthermore we had to tack to keep well clear of Cape Farewell. The only time we had been knocked down was a full 140 miles south of this so-called 'Cape of Storms', and I was anxious to avoid a repetition.

In time the wind moderated and in poor visibility we were able once again to work slowly northwards towards Cape Desolation on the south-west corner of Greenland when, without warning, dead ahead, a big iceberg loomed out of the mist. The helmsman practically threw the wheel at me; we barely squeezed by. Chastened, we continued on and into the Davis Strait.

I had a crew of four on board: Jacko, a former pupil of Kingham Hill School who had done quite a lot of sailing, some of it with me when I was still at the school, but in more temperate latitudes; two Australians, who had come over especially for this trip, one of whom, Laurie, was my relative through the marriage of my son, David, to his wife's sister. The other Australian, Steve, had never sailed before, and the Atlantic proved something of a test; whenever it got rough, Steve got sick. Laurie occasionally suffered but they both still got out of their bunks and stood their watches. Dudley completed the crew as mate, an experienced sailor, but this was to be his first Atlantic passage.

Some of the younger members of the crew seemed to suffer from this strange modern fetish of continually drinking water. This was fine except that, just as small boats do not carry unlimited supplies of diesel, nor do they of fresh water, and we were running low. But here in the Davis Strait we solved the problem temporarily by launching the rubber dinghy, and Jacko, one of the chief water drinkers, and Laurie, rowed around and scooped up bits of brash which had broken off a nearby iceberg. These we melted down on the stove. It sounds easy, but in fact even quite small lumps of ice are heavy. It was important that the ice came from an iceberg and not pack ice, because icebergs calve from glaciers and are therefore formed of fresh water from inland, whereas pack ice is frozen sea water. We enjoyed lacing our celebratory drams with 25,000-year-old glacier ice.

Our first port of call was the former cod-fishing centre of Paamiut where we replenished our dwindling supplies of fuel and water. Paamiut is well protected, and notable for the wreck of a large vessel sitting upright to starboard of the narrow fjord leading to the settlement and harbour. Picking up fuel was easy here as there was a hose that could be extended down and across to the boat; water on the other hand was more difficult and was only available by joining hoses together at the Royal Arctic Shipping wharf.

Paamiut lies approximately 160 miles south of the capital Nuuk, where we renewed acquaintance with various people we had got to know in 1998: Anders, the Greenland Danish MP, and Peter, the harbourmaster of the yacht club, who had done much of the repair work for us after our knock down.

From Nuuk we pursued our course up the Davis Strait and in turn the wind played its usual Greenlandic trick of either blowing a near gale or dying to a flat calm. Following the only line of soundings shown on the Danish chart we entered the long Kangerdluarssuqssuaq Fjord, and then at the far end ran aground on the silt bank which extends well out from the river at its head. Gunning the engine, we turned, slid off and anchored in a more reasonable depth.

Climbing and reconnaissance

Our purpose for reaching the head of this 15-mile-long fjord was to climb some of the prominent peaks which towered above it. Dudley stayed on the boat and the two Australians and myself set out. We quickly learned that this is big country, and the only available maps are woefully inadequate, at least for mountaineering. On the 1:250,000 Saga maps the slopes appear as an even, uniform ascent. But the contour lines are spaced every 100 metres of height apart, giving plenty of room for dips and rises in between. And on a small-scale map like this it is often difficult to get an idea of the considerable distances involved. It was a long and eventful ascent up the glacial valley towards our chosen peak.

Clouds of midges greeted us at the start by the river. Wisely the Australians had brought hats with midge netting. Faces and heads enclosed, they looked like Martians. Living on the west coast of Scotland I was more accustomed to the little blighters. Farther up we topped a rise and there in the dip below, as surprised as we were, stood some caribou. Laurie found a full set of antlers and plonked them on his head. I told him he looked better like that.

Steve, who was more used to climbing than sailing, headed the clamber up the steep side of the mountain, some of which was outright rock climbing. It seemed to go on and on until the ridge was attained. This ridge also carried on for a long way, but finally led on to the summit of nearly 500 metres which, much to the delight of the Australians who had not made the first ascent of a mountain before, we reached that evening. With the national flag held above their heads for the summit photo, we named the peak *Aussie Peak* in their honour. How that is going to be translated into Greenlandic is another matter.

The way back was long and arduous, especially for the old man who trailed behind. It was not until the early hours that he rejoined the youngsters who had been waiting patiently on the shore by the dinghy, which we then had to drag through the soft silt before we could launch it and row back to the boat. Sleep at last.

Before we left we climbed another peak at some 340 metres. This is an area of well-defined peaks and the challenge is more one of finding the route, often over loose or broken rock, rather than technical climbing. This was an impressive looking peak: the boat immediately below looked tiny. There were others around; we hoped to return one day.

The pilotage on the way north was just as 'interesting', avoiding hidden rocks especially round the end of one of the islands. At Ilulissat we began to shed crew. The plan was for one lot to sail the boat across the Atlantic, and for another crew of crack climbers to join us in Greenland for the next major project: the big wall climb of *Sandersons Hope*. Dudley and Jacko left us in Ilulissat, and Laurie and Steve stayed on and helped sail the boat round to Qaasut with its airstrip, on the northern side of Nuussuaq, where they left. I still have this vision of Steve rushing up the beach in an outpouring of relief at being on land and off the boat at last. To my knowledge the poor fellow has never sailed again. I'm afraid the Atlantic did it for him big time.

The pretty harbour of Uummannaq Island, with its underwater chain across the mouth to stop icebergs floating in, became our base. We would pick up the next crew from Qaasut to save the extortionate helicopter fee from there to Uummannaq. The first pair to come out were Graham, a Brit, and his Austrian girlfriend, Geli. As they had come out some two weeks ahead of the Italians Paolo and Alberto, who were to join us for the big wall climb later, we thought we might as well head north and reconnoitre the climb rather than wait around. So we made our way 150 miles north to the Upernavik region and surveyed the formidable rock wall of *Sandersons Hope*, and some possible anchorages.

On its north side *Sandersons Hope* presents an impressive wall of gneiss rock, unclimbed at that stage, of some 900 metres. The Elizabethan explorer John Davis named the island after his 'sponsor' in England, William Sanderson, and it is generally agreed that it was from here that Davis fixed his point of departure from Greenland on his, albeit unsuccessful, search for the Northwest Passage.

Pleased with our survey, we returned first to Uummannaq harbour and then to Qaasut where we toiled on foot up the steep hill to the airport to collect Paolo and Alberto. The Italians' climbing gear was packed in barrels which we carried and rolled down to the boat. Thanks to a stiff breeze we were all soaked by the time the five of us plus gear had dinghied out to *Dodo*, but we weighed anchor there and then, with our sights set on Upernavik.

The breeze died and we motored steadily across the huge 40 mile open mouth of Uummannaq Fjord towards the Svartenhuk peninsula throughout that afternoon and the light-as-day night. Next morning the wind increased rapidly and I came on deck to find Graham struggling to steer. We reefed the main, turned off the engine and tacked out to avoid an outlying reef off Svartenhuk. Geli had never even set foot on a boat before and when in the teeth of the gale she came up for her watch, she was so terrified that for the first 20 minutes on deck she could do nothing but stand stock still.

Reaching with triple-reefed main we bashed on and when we eventually reached the headland of Svartenhuk we found some protection from the cliffs. At the next headland the wind was swirling all over the place and when it gusted up to 51 and 56 knots I decided enough was enough. We dropped our sails, lay a-hull and drifted.

The climbers among us were distraught. They could see land and they wanted to be on it. I tried to explain that in a gale we would be 'much safer out to sea where there is less to bump into'. I had been steering for a while and, by now too tired to explain further, I flopped down on my bunk and was asleep before my head hit the pillow. The Italians had been confined to theirs since the gale broke.

Thirty minutes later I woke up and bowed to the inevitable. I fired up the engine and steering slightly off the wind and dodging waves as best I could, we inched towards the coast. After what felt like an eternity and despite my scepticism ('I have to tell you I don't think this is going to work') we entered a U-shaped harbour which I had discovered on an earlier exploit. The harbour is formed by a massive gravel breakwater – most likely an ancient terminal moraine.

Open to the east, the bay offered little hope of shelter in the south-easterly gale, but we found a little curve on its southern side where we could tuck in out of the wind. We dropped our anchor: 40 metres of chain in 4 metres of depth, with an 'angel' (basically a heavy weight) lowered down the chain to increase the anchor's holding power. And we put down a second anchor with chain and warp. Paolo and Alberto were on deck, able once more to be of use and with that I organised an anchor watch, dropped on to my bunk and slept. I woke four hours later to flat calm. Next stop? Upernavik.

Sandersons Hope

No route had been climbed on the north face of *Sandersons Hope*. It was to be a direct ascent of the prime line up the huge sweeping compact gneiss wall, involving some 900 metres of highly technical, specialised climbing. This area is studded with big walls and sweeping climbs in dramatic fjords, all hitherto unknown and undeveloped. *Sandersons Hope* is the biggest wall in the region and we hoped that achieving such a significant ascent would open up the area for climbers in the future.

We had a back-up team of two (me and Geli), and an international team of star climbers: Graham, Paolo, Alberto, all qualified Alpine guides, ready to break new ground.

To start the climb we had first to nose the bow of the boat right up to the cliff dropping sheer into the sea and then Alberto, our tallest member, stepped from the pulpit, the protective rail at the bow of the boat, on to the rock wall. Just above was a ledge, which the team gained and used as a base for all their gear for the next and most testing stage: nearly a kilometre of hard rock climbing. But this was not as straightforward as it might sound. A third of the way up they came to a completely blank section with absolutely no holds on the rock at all. They had to resort to a technique which climbers normally try to avoid but is sometimes necessary on a big wall such as this one: the only way that the team could make progress through this section was by drilling some bolts into the cliff.

Our original plan had been for the team to climb halfway up, fixing ropes behind them as they went so they could abseil down in the evening and return to the boat for food and sleep, before jumaring back up the ropes the next day. Then from halfway they were going to set up portaledges – a tent with a built-in 'ledge' which can be folded and stuffed in bags for hauling up the cliff face, then sprung open and suspended from cams or chocks slotted into cracks in the wall – and thus stay for the rest of the climb on the cliff face itself. However, they so enjoyed coming down to the boat in the evening and then being motored round to our anchorage for a meal and a sound night's sleep on board that they continued to fix ropes farther and farther up the cliff for about 800 metres before making a final push.

The team's change of plan turned out to be for the best. In Greenland, the summer of 2000 was strangely poor and the climbing was continually interrupted by bad weather. Sometimes the climbers had to wait, frustrated, on the boat for two or three days before the weather cleared and the rock dried out. Indeed, on the final day they woke to find the face plastered with snow and ice high up, but decided to go for the final push regardless. By now darkness was creeping into the Arctic nights and it was only by climbing well into the night and in icy conditions that the task was achieved.

Towards the top, severely hampered by ice, Paolo was forced to use artificial climbing methods. Having run out of gear he placed a stone as a chock in an icy crack and put a sling around it, but as he stepped up onto the sling the chock stone pinged out of the crack and he fell a full 10 metres before the rope stopped him. In spite of all the difficulties that the team had to overcome, late that dark night came the message, 'We have made the top, and are on the way down'. When they finally arrived, their weary faces illuminated by the head torches strapped to their helmets, there was much rejoicing. The champagne we had saved to celebrate this great occasion was cold. We popped the cork and proposed a toast to *Sandersons Hope* and us.

My team of international stars had broken new ground. They had made the first ascent of the north wall of *Sandersons Hope* at 72°43'N, completing it at 2300 hrs on 8 September, 2000. We named the route *Arctic First Born* and it was graded E3, 5c (British), A3+ in rock climbing terms; E standing for Extreme.

The next day dawned clear and sunny, which was exactly what we needed because the team now had to walk back up to the top and then abseil down the huge wall 'cleaning' the climb of any gear that they had left on the ascent. The cleaning took two days to complete and then it was time to go. The nights were by now dark for a good six hours so henceforth we would usually anchor overnight – the risk of failing to see ice was not worth taking. The passage south, however, was not without incident.

An evening and a day motoring in gentle conditions found us at the U-shaped harbour where we had sheltered from the gale. On our approach I was on watch, sitting on the gas bottle at the stern writing postcards, when several local dories with powerful outboards came up astern. Then began a duck-shooting fest, first in the fjord and then inside the anchorage where the whizzing bullets sometimes felt far too close for comfort. The locals were stocking up on meat for the winter and it seemed they had no intention of starving. The ducks did not stand a chance, although some had a brief reprieve when Graham and Geli joined one of the dories and Graham 'helped' with the shooting.

Duck shooting aside, we needed to stay on schedule and there were planes to catch. The barometer was plummeting, the weatherfax refused to spit out any synoptic charts and, with six hours of darkness to factor in, we had to decide whether or not we should put out to cross the 40-mile-wide iceberg- and growler-ridden Uummannaq Fjord.

The wind died in the afternoon and I decided to make a mad dash for it. First we motored, then as the wind steadily increased we motor-sailed and then sailed, and we avoided ice. All this we did under cloudless skies despite the plunging barometer. When it became dark we rigged a spotlight and doubled the watches, but what really saved us that night was the full moon and the lack of brash ice between the growlers and bergs. Paolo and Alberto, still inexperienced sailors, were surprised to be standing night watches together but on their own, but I was weary and felt I could trust them to cope.

The wind was gaining strength and we were piling along at a great rate on the final approaches to Nuussuaq when, suddenly, dead ahead our way was barred by a big field of brash ice and heaving growlers broken off nearby icebergs. I ran to the mast and dragged down the mainsail while Graham and Geli took the helm and steered to avoid what could have been instant disaster. It was white knuckle concentration, but they never lost it and brought us through undamaged. Brilliant. But our nerves were jangling.

Rounding the point in a full gale we aimed straight for the protective lee of a headland where we threw the anchor over, and as usual dived into our bunks as soon as it was settled. At times such as this our mentor Bill Tilman would have come out with a well-chosen proverb. 'Fortune favours the brave', perhaps. Truth be told, in this case, for 'brave' read 'foolish' – again.

There was no room for complacency and next day heading down the Vaigat Channel we encountered yet more strong wind and yet more ice. The Vaigat runs between Disko Island and the mainland and it is dramatic, with steep, snow-covered peaks sweeping along both sides. But we had our eyes fixed on the water ahead, avoiding the ice. Next morning the barometer had soared and yet we woke to falling snow. Sometimes there is no understanding weather in these parts, except to know that it can be unpredictable.

And so on to Ilulissat where skipper and crew began to say goodbye. Paolo and Alberto flew home immediately – the Italian climbers were another pair who positively shot off the boat, so keen were they to touch dry land. Graham and Geli helped me sail the boat across Disko Bay to Aasiaat, then they, too, were gone. I left as soon as I had *Dodo* lifted out for the winter and had stored my gear in the boat shed, ready for the next adventure.

What should it be? The boat was in Greenland. Things had gone well and it was a novel way of doing things, combining sailing and climbing. So, inspired by Bill Tilman's example, I decided to continue with sailing to climb, but this time to focus on ski mountaineering first ascents and traverses.

ARCTIC AGAIN AND THE TILMAN TRAVERSE

O Lord, when Thou givest to thy servants to endeavour any great matter, grant us also to know that it is not the beginning, but the continuing of the same until it be thoroughly finished that yields the true glory...

SIR FRANCIS DRAKE

In June the next year I returned to Aasiaat and put *Dodo's Delight* back in the water. I had spent some time that winter ski instructing in Villars, and much of the rest of it (as usual in the winter before an expedition) was taken up with preparations. In spite of an untimely strike by Greenland Air the crew joined me in the first week of July. Brian (a fellow boat owner) was signed up as mate, and he would look after *Dodo* while the rest of us were climbing. The other members of the crew – Andy, Matt and Peter (Maxi) – all worked or had worked at Aiglon College, an international boarding school in Villars in Switzerland. Fit young men in their late twenties and thirties, climbing and skiing was part of their work at the school. It promised to be a good team.

To have any hope of success our Tilman-type expedition, sailing and climbing in remote regions, needed careful planning. Bill Tilman must have been a tough old bird. In 1963, from his beloved boat *Mischief*, he and his climbing partner, Bruce Reid, who is still very much alive today, traversed north to south across Bylot Island, north of Baffin Island. Today it is hard to imagine how Tilman and Reid managed to carry fifteen days' food (including sixteen tins of pemmican, a nutritious, concentrated mix of fat and protein) plus the heavy camping and climbing equipment of the day, on foot, to make their mountainous 84-kilometre trek. We intended to make the same traverse, but on skis. First, however, we had to get there.

We studied the ice charts on the internet before we left and from the boat's weatherfax (a useful piece of kit both for weather and ice information) via Resolute. The charts show the concentration of ice in a particular area in tenths – 2/10ths, 3/10ths and so forth; 4–5/10ths would be pushing it in a small boat, especially in a glassfibre boat such as ours. Other information includes the size, thickness and age of ice floes; more detailed, but once you have learned how to interpret it, useful stuff.

We knew that the pack ice which forms right across Baffin Bay in the winter would not have cleared from the Greenland coast near the top in Melville Bay this early in the summer. There was no hope yet of getting across to Bylot Island on the Canadian side. But the ice chart did show that the ice had cleared from Uummannaq Fjord just to the north, so we made preparations to go for some remote unclimbed 2000-metre summits on the edge of the Greenland ice cap, and farther inland from the rock peaks we had climbed at Akuliarusinguaq three years earlier. Fully prepared, we set sail and quickly discovered again why Greenlanders all have motorboats: there is either too much wind or, often, too little. We had to motor to and then across the open mouth of Uummannaq Fjord to Ingia Fjord. Here we dodged the usual band of icebergs, growlers and brash ice that feeds down from a number of glaciers at the northern end of Uummannaq Fjord, and finally put in to the bay of Puartdlarsivik. We repeated our trick of hitting the steeply shelving soft alluvial silt bank with the keel – at least that way we knew exactly how deep it was – and anchored close into the northern shore of the bay.

The problem with ascending mountains by ski in Greenland in the summer is that you first have to carry all your equipment, skis, boots, food, camping and other gear to the glacier or snowline, and distances in Greenland are great. It took a horrendous two and a half days to walk in, carrying everything on our backs. We started up the long river valley and pitched our tents for the first daylight 'night' on a grassy knoll. Then we crossed a raging torrent via an ice bridge at the snout of a glacier, scrambled up a 100-metre rock slab, over lateral and terminal moraines of rocks and rubble, before finally making camp again in a small break in the boulder fields with a stream nearby – all the while carrying our fearsomely heavy rucksacks.

On the morning of the third day we reached the main approach glacier. We ascended its snout, and then swapped our crampons for skis and skins. What a relief, and we were heading into new territory. I cannot begin to describe the feeling of setting foot somewhere where no one has ever been before. We knew the Inuit would, over the centuries, never have bothered to come up here simply because there were no caribou to hunt. With skins on our skis, which made for a much easier rhythmic motion than crampons, we toiled up the glacier towards the spot we had chosen to pitch our tents.

Andy and Matt had beaten us to it, and sat smirking at the entrance to their tent, stripped down for sunbathing. They were drinking tea as Maxi and I struggled up the last few hundred metres. But they were gracious enough to offer us a cup. We levelled out a platform in the snow and ice, pitched our own tent, cooked our evening meal, and fell into our sleeping bags.

Bearing in mind our aim to climb virgin summits by ski mountaineering, Andy and Matt set off to look for one marked on the Saga map some distance away to the north. The summits here on the edge of the Greenland ice cap are rounded snow domes rather than well-defined peaks, and in the uniform terrain Andy and Matt had some difficulty finding the location of the spot-height marked on the map. They returned disconsolate, not being quite sure whether they had reached the actual 'summit' or not. They took in another possible summit on the way back as compensation. Maxi and I fared rather better and on a long, exacting day managed to ski up five previously unclimbed summits. It was complicated terrain. Map reading, and finding the highest point of the snow domes with the altimeters on our watches, was difficult. Perhaps we were being too pernickety as to the exact highest point in this rounded terrain.

While Maxi and I were ticking off a summit we had missed the day before we found ourselves on a snow bridge, with the mouth of a crevasse yawning below us, with the imminent danger of it collapsing. A split second decision: 'Shall we rope up?' 'No, keep moving!' I cried. We checked out our wayward summit, working out its height from our GPS as no spot-height was indicated on the map, and then enjoyed a magnificent ski down a steep slope of powder snow on the way back to our tent. The final slope back to camp was awkward, and with a real danger of more hidden crevasses, we did rope up, though we certainly needed more practice skiing together this way. Andy and Matt meantime had made a definite ascent of a much more prominent peak, and so altogether we had claimed six virgin summiits.

We broke camp and began the trek back to the boat. Before crossing a fast-flowing glacial stream I started to swing my rucksack over before me. A change of mind halfway, a half-hearted throw, and the sack containing all my gear and sleeping bag plopped into the stream, and started rapidly floating away on the torrent. Only Maxi's quick thinking, by rushing along the bank and grabbing it before it disappeared forever down a hole in the glacier where the stream disappeared, saved the day. To have lost all my gear would have been a disaster both for me and the expedition.

It took less time to get back as we discovered a better way, and we were spurred on by the fact that we were running out of food. But by the end I was definitely suffering from Tilman's 'mountaineer's foot' – the difficulty of putting one foot in front of the other – and the younger men were down long before the old man. Then Matt and Andy, hot and sweaty, stripped off and dived from the boat into the icy water. A photo I have shows Matt holding onto a bergy bit with one hand and waving with the other. Rather him than me.

We had a rest day, filled up with water from a mountain stream and left for Upernavik, putting in to the Sortehul channel for some climbing on the way – an area that was to become something of a mecca for our climbers in the future. We put up two new rock routes, and the old man was persuaded to follow up an extreme rock pitch, which was a bit of a shock. And then abseiling into and walking down a snow gully in tight rock shoes proved excruciatingly painful.

Upernavik and the passage across

Upernavik had an airstrip and we could make crew changes there. Maxi was staying, but Andy and Matt had to fly home, and Polly and Tashy flew out. Tilman had one cardinal rule: 'no women on board'. He once forgot to say that in his usual appeal for crew in *The Times*, and had to write to the sixteen girls who applied saying 'no' to each of them. But as already remarked, Polly and Tashy were hugely experienced, and even Tilman might have relented. Brian's wife Pat also joined us here, so that the two of them could sail *Dodo's Delight* round to Pond Inlet, while the rest of us attempted ski traverses across Bylot Island.

By coincidence, before we left Upernavik an all-Irish crew (including a friend, Paddy Barry) arrived in *Northabout*, a specially-built aluminium boat in which they were going to attempt the North West Passage. What characters they were! First they held a ceilidh in the local hostelry, singing and dancing well into the early hours, and the next evening they took over the town square – no more than a wooden platform in front of the Danish-built hospital – and entertained us with Irish fiddle, guitar and song, to the bemusement of the local population.

It was now approaching the end of July, and the ice chart showed that the band of pack ice – Middle Pack, or West Ice as the Greenlanders call it – that sticks stubbornly to the shore in the far north-west of Greenland, sometimes for the whole summer, was beginning to ease away at the northern end of Melville Bay. We might now be able to get over the top to Bylot Island. We took our departure, first filling with water from a stream on one of the nearby islands. Maxi lost a lot of marks here by dropping the old Seagull outboard engine into the water while transferring it from dinghy to boat. It never worked again.

As we sailed and motored northwards in order to get round the top of the pack ice, with wind on the nose and a rather nasty short, sharp chop, we met *Northabout* approaching from the south-east. We were surprised to see them as they had left before us, but they had stopped to climb the Devil's Thumb, a tower of rock on one of the islands. They had something for us: in the friendly to-ing and fro-ing between boats in Upernavik, Polly had left her camera behind. Now at 75°30'N they were able to motor alongside and hand over this crucial item. We waved each other farewell, and they veered off to the north-west heading for Thule and Qaanaq, while we turned south-west for Bylot Island. Later we heard that they had made it successfully through the North West Passage and in one summer – an unusual and considerable achievement in those days.

The mountains of Bylot Island lay ahead. What looked like the shoreline on the radar resolved itself into a huge band of heavy pack ice stretching far out from the shore. The ice chart suggested it was 2/10ths ice. 'If that's 2/10ths ice I'm a Dutchman,' I thought; and we were still 30 miles or more out from the coast. Tashy climbed the mast to the spreaders to search for leads. It was fruitless, but the crew were still surprised when the skipper swung the boat around and put out to sea. I knew it would be wiser to drift up and down with the tidal currents off the edge of the pack, rather than risk damage. We kept a watch during the night, slept in our clothes as usual, and bided our time.

After drifting up and down off the heaving, steaming pack for two nights and a day, the ice chart for Bylot Island showed possible access farther south. We motored with some care, especially as it was misty, and were eventually able to hold a more westerly course. Through scattered ice floes, with auks, Arctic skuas and terns much in evidence, and in beautiful, calm conditions we could now make good progress. However, in the evening, while heading towards the coast, we were halted yet again by a broad band of pack ice. We were forced to stop and reconcile ourselves to another night of drifting.

Next day the ice chart, and indeed our own eyes, revealed a more hopeful route farther south still. We made another attempt to reach the island, and were rewarded this time, anchoring in a pleasant bay in ice-free water to the south of Cape Walter Bathurst. The sun shone and a stream nearby promised fresh water. We went ashore, lit our camping stoves to test them before the traverses, and I decided to try our newly acquired shotgun. In Greenland you can buy a rifle or shotgun over the counter; this one had been found on Nuuk's rubbish dump by one of *Northabout*'s crew and, concerned at our lack of firearms in case we encountered polar bears, they had given it to us. But I was not wholly confident about this shotgun from a rubbish dump, especially as the metal parts seemed rather loosely attached to the wooden bits. Setting up a pile of stones as a target and attaching a long piece of string to pull the trigger, I propped the gun up and from a safe distance pulled the cord. The gun fired perfectly. The next cartridge I fired boldly from the shoulder, knocking over a few of the target stones. We had a working shotgun.

In the meantime, Polly had brought her sleeping bag up on deck to dry out in the sun and fresh air. Nonchalantly tossing it over the gantry at the stern, the bag caught in the whirring blades of the wind generator. She pulled it down as fast as she could in a blizzard of eiderdown.

Next morning I looked out and was surprised to see ice floes drifting rapidly by the portlight. Pack ice was piling into the bay. This looked serious. We pushed and shoved with the big sweeps given to us by the Iona Community's outdoor centre in Scotland for just such a purpose. We were desperate to keep a space open for the boat among the floes. If the skipper looked worried, the women appeared calm, and wearing only their sponsored thermal underwear, jumped down on to an ice floe for a photo shoot. The firm that supplied the gear must have been delighted.

Fortunately, as the morning progressed the ice relented, and with more pushing and shoving, and weaving and dodging on the engine, we were able to retrieve our anchor and make our way out to open water. It had been a tense experience – for me at least. It made one wonder how the old sailors had managed in these waters without engines, and it was easy to understand why many men lost their lives.

Next day after keeping careful watch overnight, drifting around in open water, we were able to make our way along the coast northwards to Cape Liverpool where Tilman had set out on his traverse across Bylot Island. A little farther on we rounded a small headland to an indentation in the coastline, which at least gave the impression of being a more sheltered anchorage.

The Bylot Island traverses

At Bylot Island, Maxi and I would repeat Tilman's traverse, but on skis, making first ascents of mountains as we went. The girls were going to make a new north-south traverse, also making first ascents, and would set out from this anchorage near Cape Liverpool. We had found polar bear paw prints in the mud ashore here so we decided that Polly and Tashy had better take the shotgun. To help with the initial carry-in of heavy rucksacks Brian had gone with the girls as far as the first glacier and should have been back at the boat by now. Time dragged through the evening and we waited and watched the shoreline. The night wore on and Pat and Maxi went ashore to look for him. No luck.

Still we waited, but it was not until much later the next day that Brian reappeared on the beach, exhausted but unharmed. Walking through featureless terrain on his way back from the glacier he had lost all sense of direction, and compasses are unreliable at these latitudes. He claimed to have passed only 100 metres away from a polar bear, but we knew that he must have been hallucinating by then. We were mightily relieved to see him alive, but drained by his ordeal he would be unable to help Maxi and I carry in our gear when the time came.

Back at Cape Liverpool we anchored by the river where Tilman had started his traverse. Rather than struggle in the confines of the boat Maxi and I packed our rucksacks on the beach where we left them propped up and ready for the off. Next morning, our backs laden with our excessively heavy rucksacks carrying skis, boots, climbing gear, tent, food, and even sleds for use on the glaciers, we set out and walked for 9 kilometres across the tundra. It nearly killed me, carrying all that weight.

As we walked we passed fresh polar bear prints. Tashy and Polly had the shotgun. We were vulnerable. We scanned 360 degrees round, could see no bear, and so we slogged on.

That night we camped by a stream not far from the start of the glacier. Blessed relief! Next morning as I heaved on my sack it felt even heavier and more burdensome than before and plodding wearily over the tundra I was thinking that if it went on like this I wasn't going to make it. But we reached the glacier, and now we could shed the weight off our backs. We snapped on our skis and strapped the rucksacks onto the sleds. It was a revelation: with skis and sticks in rhythm we worked our way with relative ease up the glacier. The skins on the undersides of our skis gripped the ice as we pulled our sleds behind us, in reality no more than glorified toboggans, but now carrying all the weight. We made good progress and by evening were only a little way below the first col leading to the next glacier. Under a warm sun we set up camp by a glacial stream.

But we had a rude shock when we topped the col in the morning. There was no snow on the sunny south-facing slope and with sacks and sleds again on our backs we laboured down over rock and scree. Once we reached the glacier, skiing again on snow and ice, we fell again into the glorious rhythm of gliding and climbing and so it continued over the next col. And here our cunning plan to stop the sleds banging against our legs on downhill runs came into its own: we threaded the ropes pulling them through stiff plastic tubing – stripped from the boat's guardrails – which we then bound together in an X-shape for added strength, and the stiff tubing prevented the sleds from trying to overtake us.

The air was crisp and clear, the sun was shining and all around us as far the eye could see, stretched magnificent snow-covered mountains. There was every reason to believe that Maxi and I, and Polly and Tashy somewhere to the west of us, were the only human presence in this vast, unspoiled, primordial land. It was good to be alive.

For ten days Maxi and I worked steadily southwards making first ascents of peaks as we went. We skied up whenever we could, and when we could not ski we climbed in alpine style. Crossing the wide, rip-roaring glacial streams challenged both our nerve and our ingenuity. Sometimes we found a snow bridge; we would inch over, one man at a time, only hoping it would hold. When there was no bridge, one man would take both ice axes and jump across the stream, ramming them into the bank to hold himself fast, then haul the sleds over, and then throw back the axes for the next man's jump. It was a laborious operation but it worked, although Maxi did lose his grip once and his feet took a soaking, to his annoyance.

The borrowed skins on Maxi's borrowed skis were beginning to disintegrate so from time to time we had to stop and stitch them back together, but despite delays we progressed steadily higher and higher, stringing the glaciers together. One night we would pitch the tent in the middle of a glacier by a fresh-water lake, on another we might camp on a ridge and see in the middle of the night the sun low on the horizon, the sky lit with its muted colours.

When towards the southern end of the island we reached the highest of the glaciers we skied up one final summit. It had a curious rock *nunatuk*, or tower, at the top but Maxi was past caring; he had been having a tough day and was no longer enjoying the climbing. I assured him that we would make no more ascents. The going should be all downhill from here we thought, as we pitched camp below on the open glacier.

The next day's skiing was straightforward and we were soon down on the long Sermilik glacier, which Tilman had used to reach the southern shore of the island. But in the evening we hit a nasty broken section riddled with crevasses where our sleds constantly jammed and tipped over, forcing us to stop, turn around, step back and right them. Fed up and frustrated I called a halt. We found a patch of flat ice between two streams, pitched the tent and brewed up.

We were tired, but even so our sleep was disturbed: the glacier creaked and the crevasses boomed. But such sleep as we managed had refreshed us and come the morning we skied on in good heart. As we neared the glacier's end one of Maxi's skins finally gave up the ghost altogether. The other soon followed suit and on the knobbly icy surface skiing without skins was no mean feat.

Tilman and his companion Bruce Reid found themselves stranded when first they reached Bylot Island's southern shore. They lit fires and made smoke as planned, so that the crew on their boat at Pond Inlet on the Baffin side would see it and come for them. For four days the smoke signals went unseen and the explorers were finally rescued by an Inuit in a canoe powered, much to Tilman's disgust, by an outboard. Wise after the event, Maxi and I were carrying a small VHF, although Pond Inlet seemed a long way off and I did wonder if we would get through.

But Polly answered our call immediately. They had been on their way over even before we radioed, 'just in case'. We made a double-quick descent of the final steep icy slope on to the beach and this time I could not be bothered to unhitch and then carry the sled and sack on my back; dragging it over the boulders was good enough for me. Polly and Tashy came to fetch us in the dinghy and delighted, congratulatory hugs and kisses were the happy conclusion to ten days, 80 kilometres and the eight first ascents we had achieved while following in the footsteps of Bill Tilman.

The girls in the meantime had completed their groundbreaking north-south route in eight days and we named it the *Murray-Wright Traverse*. When they reached the south shore, however, they had no VHF and, in any event, because the weather conditions were poor, the boat could not come for them. They had no choice but to sit it out. After two days all they had left to eat between them was one square of chocolate, and they were getting ready to start trying to shoot sea birds to eat when Brian and Pat arrived in *Dodo*.

Polly and Tashy had run low on food during their long 90-kilometre traverse and were thus compelled to keep going apace with no time to climb any peaks. But any twinges of disappointment there may have been on my side were as nothing compared to the achievement. The *Murray-Wright Traverse* had been added to the map and honour was satisfied.

Homeward bound

We were all safely together and back on board *Dodo* in Pond Inlet. Throughout the week we spent there, Louis and Charmain, a Royal Canadian Mounted Police couple in Pond, took us under their wing. They invited us to supper almost every evening, and Charmain made a delicious chocolate cake for Polly's birthday. We re-stocked the boat, filled up with diesel and encouraged by the ice chart – no pack ice at all in Baffin Bay – set a direct course for Upernavik. At sea, in the galley, a hungry crew opened one of the tins of chicken we had bought and found, fair enough, a chicken, but with its head, beak, legs and even a few feathers.

In only four days we were at Upernavik where we left Pat to catch her flight home and back to work. Polly was returning to Scotland from Ilulissat, 250 miles farther south, and in order to get there on the day she was due to fly, we had to first motorsail with a Force 5, 6 and occasionally 7 bang on the nose, and then to weave through big fields of ice driven north from the huge glacier at Ilulissat. We arrived in time for Polly to leap from boat to taxi to airport to check-in, and she made the flight, but only just. Then Jessy came out and joined us for the passage home.

Rolling south down the Davis Strait before a strong following wind, which died to nothing and then rose again, we sailed and motored according to its mood, before finally closing the coast for shelter and rest. That evening we anchored off the ruins of an old Moravian mission in a small inlet off a fjord. There was a large cemetery nearby where some of the ancient Inuit graves – no more than shallow depressions covered with rocks – had broken open revealing the all too visible skulls and skeletons within.

Next day before setting out on the next leg we replenished our stores at the settlement of Qeqertarsuatsiaq (Fiskenaesset) farther along the fjord, and then slipped gently through the sheltered passage inside the islands. Tashy and Jessy were on the bridge deck sketching and painting the unfolding landscape: in mirror-clear water there floated into view a small berg, then a growler, and the hills beyond rose stark and still. Tashy held up a sketch, 'What do you think, Bob?' 'That's good,' I said. A pause before she cried, 'No, look, it's hopeless. This line isn't right; the perspective is out here, and here...' Artistic temperament? It looked very good to me.

Tropical storms generally track out into the Atlantic, but the tail end of Erin was skimming the Greenland coast and as soon as we were sailing in more open water we had to duck inside the island of Ravns Storø to avoid its full force. The enclosed bay we entered had, interestingly, been a Faroese fishing harbour, but was now a scene of dereliction. The wooden fishermen's huts had all collapsed, their scattered timbers left to rot. No trees grow in Greenland because of the winter ice so wood is a scarce commodity, but there was plenty to be had here. What might be termed twentieth-century industrial and domestic artefacts littered the ground – cookers, sinks and toilets and all the detritus of an erstwhile thriving summer harbour. I spent a lot of time and energy at the old jetty removing a big balk of timber with plenty of nails from under the waterline which I thought might scour *Dodo*'s hull.

After being gale-bound for thirty-six hours, we set off for Paamiut. On the way we passed close to the massive Fredrikshaab Isblink glacier. Nearly 5 kilometres wide, it is also unusual in having a sandy shoreline stretching the length of its long foot.

Paamiut was our last chance to stock up the boat before crossing the Atlantic. It is reputedly the 'worst town in Greenland', although we have never found it so. In Paamuit we first heard the news that had sent shockwaves around the world. Two policemen had asked to see our passports. We handed them over, but in easy-going Greenland it was unusual to be asked for documentation and when I asked the officers why, they said, 'Since the Twin Towers we have to do this'. 'What Twin Towers?' we asked. We had been at sea for a week and it was now 18 September. We had until now been totally oblivious to 9/11.

Among the people we met by the harbour was an elderly sea captain who was restoring an old wooden boat, unusual these days in Greenland. And with the ship's stores replenished and with caribou meat, Arctic cod and crab on board as gifts from the sea captain, we departed from Paamiut at 0620 on 20 September, which was rather late in the year to set sail across the Atlantic.

Atlantic crossing

Boat and crew were ready for our Atlantic passage but when we set out, to keep well clear of another tropical storm, Gabrielle, which was hitting Cape Farewell at the southern tip of Greenland, we first headed south and a little west. It was a bumpy ride and the nights were dark now so all the time we were also keeping a close eye on the radar in case of ice. In the Labrador Sea, at 54°27'N and well south of Cape Farewell, we tacked east towards the Atlantic proper. We had been keeping a wary eye on the weatherfax too and a tight ball of isobars to the south, but this new storm, Humberto, finally spun east straight out into the Atlantic and did not trouble us.

Then, for a while, the ship's log read 'all reefs out' and 'all plain sail'. That big yellow ball in the sky reappeared, and Tashy and Jessy grabbed at a chance to dry out their sleeping bags on deck. But all too soon the weather reverted to 'normal for this time of year'. The wind increased and our tired old mainsail was suffering, but with Tashy holding up my back to stop me falling I could stitch and repair the tears while the sail was still in place.

Here follows a tale of depressions and gales. A steadily increasing wind was the forerunner to a deep depression heading up from Newfoundland, deepening as it came until it hit an ultimate low at 957mbs which came close to the lowest I had ever seen. However, it passed well ahead of us and the strong northerlies in its wake gave us two or three days of good sailing until a secondary depression circled back and we fell into its eye.

I had read about the dead eye of depressions and the unpleasant and uncomfortable experience we had with this one concurred with the written description. In very disturbed seas and with no wind to steady us we were thrown around all over the place. I was to have much the same experience crossing the Atlantic three years later. But the eye passed and heralded a breeze, which wound up quickly to Force 5, 6 then 7, and then to Force 8/9. The boat was overpowered even under storm jib alone, and so we ran before the wind under bare poles all through the night. The seas were lively and large, but our Autosteer windvane self-steering coped magnificently. More important, the gale, for once, was pushing us the way we wanted to go.

During the morning the wind moderated to Force 5–7 and we were making good, fast progress. And so we cracked on; we were more than halfway across. But approaching 20°W longitude we were knocked back by yet another gale, this time from the wrong direction. We tried heaving-to on a backed jib, but having once before lost a mast at sea I had become perhaps over-sensitive about strain on the rigging and worried that the sheet was putting too much stress on the cap shroud. So we doused the sail and lay a-hull for 12 hours under bare poles, with the wheel lashed hard over to keep us broadside to the waves. Tashy wrote in the log in her characteristic italic script, 'Wind up and down from 19–49 knots.' It was good to know that she had not lost her sense of humour.

We attached the trysail to the boom hoping that it might give us some drive, but it hardly mattered because soon we were once again slopping around in the eye of another depression.

And then the Atlantic decided to be kind to us and the log read, 'Great sailing. Beam to close-reaching. Sun and wind.' And, 'Big cumulus and stratocumulus', harbingers of the fair weather in which we were bowling along, reefing and unreefing, towards the edge of soundings at around 10°W longitude. But again we were headed and before we were pushed too far north we tacked south towards the Rockall Bank. 'Clear night, good speed,' read the log, although as the night wore on and the wind blew harder the crew were writing, 'Wind up, 3 reefs, No. 3 jib', and then 'Trysail [sheeted to the boom] and No. 3 jib'.

'Land Ahoy,' shouted Brian next day. And the hump we were looking at was, Brian assured us, the Outer Hebridean island of Hecla, which he had good reason to identify as it was also the name of his boat. The wind backed and went astern and so we goosewinged and then broad-reached towards Pabbay. Jessy conjured up a Cornish-style cream tea from we know not where and, wearing shorts of all things, brought it up to us on deck. It was still daylight when we turned farther abeam and through the Sound of Pabbay, and so towards the islands of the Inner Hebrides. We shot across the Minch with north-westerly Force 5 and 6 on the quarter.

Darkness had fallen and rain was lashing down when off the island of Coll we passed by a trawler, all lights blazing; it was the first boat we had seen for more than 2000 miles. It was a filthy night so we headed into Tobermory, on Mull. We entered the harbour, our eyes screwed up against near-horizontal sleet, and tied up against a raft of fishing boats at the ferry pier. 'They won't be going out in this weather,' I thought. I was wrong. At 0600 they fired up their engines and *Dodo* was spattered with diesel soot and, also, a generous extra spattering of scallops for breakfast.

It had been a successful expedition in the Tilman tradition, albeit with a taxing and sometimes frustrating return passage of some 2400 miles in twenty days.

06

VARIETY IS THE SPICE OF LIFE

Boats and adventuring are expensive and to fund my way of life I worked during winters in Europe as a ski instructor. But money was always tight and when in 2002 I was offered the job of delivery skipper, I jumped at it. The first delivery was a baptism of fire but others followed. The work not only helped to pay the bills but also brought new experiences: I sailed a range of boats, met all manner of people and visited places I might not otherwise have gone to. I had a lot to learn, and I learned a lot… I also came to realise that my style of simple self-sufficient sailing, for better or worse, was not shared by some of the owners of the boats I would help to deliver. GPS, satphones, computers, shore-side weather routing and constant chatter. Where would it end?

'MUTINY' ON THE *PALANDRA*

Can you understand this, Mr. Byam? Discipline is the thing.

MUTINY ON THE BOUNTY, CAPTAIN WILLIAM BLIGH

Out of the blue Bruce, a friend of mine, phoned: 'My father has bought a Moody 52 in Florida – would you like to bring it back to Scotland for him? He'll pay you.' I did not miss a beat: 'Yes'. This, it transpired, was perhaps my first mistake but I could not help myself. The prospect was exciting and the money would help towards *Dodo*'s maintenance bills.

Across the Atlantic from Florida, USA, to Loch Sween in Scotland was to be my first 'job' as a delivery skipper. I had my RYA Yachtmasters' Offshore and Ocean certificates and that was it. Did I need any others? I had no idea but as the delivery was a private arrangement between friends I decided that pieces of paper were relatively unimportant.

Cape Canaveral to New York

In June 2002, I flew via Orlando to a very hot Cape Canaveral in Florida, enduring the expected but still horrendously long post-9/11 queues at airport security. At Cape Canaveral we found the boat, *Palandra*, in the water with her owners, Alastair and Dorothy, on board. They'd been working hard on the boat for about two weeks, but there was still much to be done. The new plotter/radar was yet to be installed, and everything in the saloon appeared to be in pieces which, added to the terrific humidity and heat, made it difficult to do any work below.

Palandra was easily solid and strong enough to withstand ocean sailing, but her interior was less impressive, at least in my opinion. For example, there were too few grab handles, there was no strap in the galley to hold one secure when stormy, the chart table was much too small and the very large windows in the deckhouse saloon would be vulnerable in a gale. We were pushed for time to complete or to properly test the work which we did manage to do on the boat, and maybe this was my second mistake.

But we were under pressure to make our departure. The owner's daughter, Carolyn, needed to be back in the north of Scotland to organise a charity ball, and flights for crew changeovers in New York in a couple of weeks' time had been booked and paid for. Dorothy returned to deal with the family business in Scotland, and so a few days after I had arrived we put out to sea. For this first passage there was Alastair and Carolyn, younger daughter Elizabeth, Bruce's wife Naomi, a family friend Ken, and myself. Big boat; large crew.

By nightfall on the first day we already had a reef in the mainsail. The boat sailed very well, but we soon found that the reefing system was far from user-friendly. Because of the high deckhouse the boom was high which made it difficult to reach and pull down the reefing rings on the luff of the sail, as Naomi and I discovered almost immediately. Later I rigged a line connecting all the rings together which made it easier to pull the sail down. During the night the wind went round so we gybed, and despite us controlling the mainsail as we did so, it split almost the length of a seam and from then on we had to keep one reef in.

The wind died and we motored round Cape Hatteras on the engine, more often a place of fearfully high seas thrown up when the Gulf Stream goes head to head with strong northerlies. The current, 4–5 knots, was rushing us helpfully northwards and as the wind still did not fill in we motored all the way to New York, up the Hudson River, past the impressive Statue of Liberty, and under the Verrazano-Narrows Bridge.

We tied up at the marina at Liberty Landings. The marina was attractive and we enjoyed fine dining at the restaurant converted from an old lightship, although I was glad I was not paying the bills. While we waited for our new crew to arrive, Alastair and various family members went out on the town and took in a Broadway show, as one does. We needed some gear for the boat and it gave me an excuse to take the ferry to Manhattan and go shopping at the West Marine chandlery on 37th Street. Walking back, I felt saddened as I passed Ground Zero. The site seemed both a terrible and poignant place, and I was especially moved by the memorial with photos of all the firemen who had died trying to save the lives of others. Yet in defiance of tragedy, the huge American flag draped from a building overlooking Ground Zero proclaimed an indomitable spirit.

We arranged to have the mainsail repaired and when the sailmaker came to collect it he also took our entire suit of sails for a thorough once-over and renewal of all the stitching that had rotted. Bright tropical sunlight is a menace when it comes to sailcloth. We also sought expert opinion on our plotter/radar, which was still not working as it should. And to stop the boom whacking hard across the boat on a gybe, I rigged up preventers that would remain permanently attached to the main boom; it seemed a good idea at the time…

New York to Newfoundland

We left New York on 22 June, 2002, to cross the Atlantic. People told us we should go north past Long Island, but we went south down the Hudson River, the quicker route out to sea. There had been quite a crew change in New York: Carolyn, Naomi, Elizabeth and Ken had all gone home, and Iain (Alastair's brother) had come out, accompanied by Frank. We were also joined by some young men: Robbie, Peter and another Alastair who was Iain's son (very confusing). Bigger ocean, larger crew. On our second night out the scene was set for "Mutiny' on the *Palandra*'.

Frank had done a fair bit of sailing, albeit offshore and only as far as St Kilda as far as I knew. He went on deck in the night and found two of the lads on watch a little too relaxed for his liking; in fact they were stretched out in the cockpit. The autopilot was on, we had quite a lot of sail up in a reasonably strong breeze, and the saloon hatches were open (but there was no spray). This led him to question the watchkeeping system – why were two relatively inexperienced youngsters on watch together? – and then by extension to criticise the running of the boat.

I agreed to re-examine the watchkeeping regime. Iain suffers from multiple sclerosis and therefore needed to be on watch with someone both competent and experienced, which was one reason why Frank had been invited to come. But the watch system as it stood was the best I could come up with and so I concluded that we should stick with it. Frank disagreed and asked to be put ashore in Halifax, which was 300 miles away. The owner, his brother and I talked it over and, agreeing that on a boat there can be only one skipper, we decided that we would indeed have to divert to Halifax. I said no more about it, although I thought the whole business had become rather overwrought.

We duly altered course for Halifax. Then I heard that Frank had not slept for three nights in harbour, the last with much drink taken, and was exhausted. After two spells off watch and having slept well, he saw things in a different light, and the night before we got to Halifax – all such negotiations seemed to take place on the night watches – he rather shamefacedly asked if he could 'stay on after all?' Well, the man could certainly sail, we were short of experienced sailors and he was immensely strong physically. So, 'Yes, as far as I was concerned' I told him, provided he remembered that I was the skipper. The owner and his brother agreed and from then on Frank and I got along famously. But our diversion reminded me of something that once happened to Bill Tilman and I knew the old man would have given us a wry smile… In his case, however, on one of his expeditions it had been two of his recalcitrant crew who insisted on leaving him in Gibraltar. Tilman continued on to South America without them and made his noteworthy crossing of the Patagonia ice cap.

So we need not have altered course to Halifax after all, but then we would have missed some rare experiences. On 26 June as we were approaching Halifax, Nova Scotia, the Canadian warship *HMCS Montreal 336* steamed past and radioed. We gave the owner's name, nationality, ship's registration and so on. Then on our VHF we heard them call a 145-foot motor vessel astern of us. There was no response. Next the warship stated her intention to steam across the vessel's bows. We could see her searchlight playing onto the motor yacht's bridge and we listened, fascinated by the lengthy exchange.

After being given the ship's details, the Canadian captain announced that they were going to board and search it. However the motor yacht's captain was reluctant to alter course to 240°, slow to 5 knots and heave-to as requested, giving reasons such as, 'We have a tight schedule and must stick to it'; 'I will have to contact my owner first'; 'I am having difficulty contacting my owner'; 'He has agreed to a search when we arrive in Boston', and even, 'This is piracy'.

The Canadians were unfazed, 'Roger that, sir, but under the agreement to which your nation is a signatory we have the right to search your vessel. I understand your concern, but I repeat, we shall be boarding your vessel this afternoon.' Finally, the Canadian captain warned the motor vessel that if they continued to refuse to heave-to he would fire medium-calibre rounds 1,000 yards in front of their vessel. There was to be a three-minute warning.

Warship 336, 'Clear the upper decks'. Then, 'Please confirm you have cleared the upper decks.'

Motor vessel, 'I have cleared the upper decks.' A burst of medium-calibre rounds illicit no response from the vessel.

Warship 336, 'If you do not heave-to within three minutes, I will fire medium-calibre rounds 500 yards in front of your vessel.'

No response. The rounds are fired.

Motor vessel, 'Gee, that was close.' But they still do not alter course to heave-to.

Warship 336, 'If you do not heave-to within three minutes I will fire heavy-calibre rounds 1,000 yards in front of your vessel.'

No response. Heavy-calibre rounds are fired at 1,000 yards.

Not until heavy-calibre rounds were fired at 500 yards did the captain of the motorboat agree to heave-to and allow the vessel to be searched.

We never learned the outcome of the search as we were by then in the approaches to Halifax and had lost contact, but I was full of admiration for the professionalism of the warship's captain and felt that, at least in these waters, there was nothing to fear. What is more, this is the only time in my life that I have ever experienced a vessel being fired at. On my inaugural delivery trip it was a particularly intriguing first.

Halifax

There were some outlying islands at the entrance to Halifax with a long, twisting estuary leading into the harbour and town, but we followed the buoys – albeit red and green are reversed on this side of the Atlantic – and once inside forked left to the Royal Nova Scotia Yacht Squadron, where I played hard on the fact that we came from old Scotia. The members were unimpressed, but they did make us very welcome. We relaxed in comfort and had a good and, unlike in New York, reasonably priced meal.

While here I also teamed up with a couple in a smart 36-foot steel sailing boat and went on a little trip with them round to the main harbour of Halifax. The boat was well maintained and fitted out, and in many ways would have been ideal for polar sailing. I wondered what I was doing with a small fibreglass boat instead; then I thought about the cost. Tied up near us was a rather quicker boat – a racing machine called *Spirit of Canada*, the Canadian entry for the forthcoming BOC (single-handed round the world sailing race). So after stocking up with food and diesel, filling our LPG gas bottles and wishing the Canadian challenger good luck (Ellen MacArthur was not competing), we set off again.

There was barely a breath of wind when we left Halifax and for the next 600 miles we motored until we stopped at St John's, Newfoundland, for yet more diesel. St John's appeared to me as Sodom or Gomorrah: 'sin city', with girls soliciting openly on the streets in the middle of the day. Frank had thumbed a lift into town and to his credit when the car stopped at a set of lights he insisted on jumping out, returning to the boat some time later with lurid tales of what had been on offer.

The stopover had its moments for me, too. Friends and fellow Greenland hands Greg and Keri on their liveaboard steel yacht *Northanger* were busy on the other side of the peninsula getting ready for a charter to Antarctica with the Commodore and some members of the Ocean Cruising Club. Keri, Greg and I spent a happy day aboard *Northanger* comparing notes about recent expeditions to Greenland and talking over plans for the future. I offered to do some varnishing for them in the heads, although Keri jokingly immediately found faults – what she called 'holidays', which meant to say I had missed bits. Members of the OCC I reckoned had more than enough skills to put that right.

That evening we met Ted Laurentius, the local OCC port officer, and his wife, Karen, and Greg and I went for a sail on their boat, *Panache*. Greg and I played holiday charter guests, drinking beer and refusing to steer or tweak any ropes, at which Karen left the helm and let the boat steer itself – which it did, beautifully. There was a nasty moment when it looked as if we might have had to exert ourselves to execute a tack, but Ted dealt with it. Beers in the sun (just the one) on a beam reach across Conception Bay was a dream.

Atlantic

The Atlantic was playing up. No wind? Almost unheard of. And thick mist? We were forced to motor for five days, passing what were almost certainly icebergs which we could not see and which showed up only on the radar. On the fourth day the autopilot packed up. Some of the young crew were comparatively inexperienced and largely because of the conditions had not had much opportunity to show interest in learning what went on in a boat. But as I have often found over the years with young people, I need not have worried. In mid-Atlantic the breeze finally filled in, and they rose to the occasion. The gales of student laughter issuing from the cockpit did however suggest a certain lack of concentration.

And then we broke the boom. Alastair who was on the helm at the time was just moving to change position in the cockpit when he was distracted by his brother Iain coming up from the saloon; there was a moment's loss of concentration, the wind got behind the sail, and whack, across went the boom and … it broke in two. Although it was Alastair, the owner, who had been on the helm, I felt guilty. It was I after all who had rigged the permanent preventers on the boom for just such an eventuality; it had broken mid-way down, at the point of attachment of the permanent preventers. However, they kindly refused to blame me. Perhaps there was already some weakness in the boom? I can only say the system has served me well for thousands of miles on my own boat.

Frank really came into his own at this point. He was a tower of strength. He managed to heave the aft broken section of the boom up alongside the other half so we could then lash them together. Though we could no longer set the mainsail, now that we had some breeze and it was abaft the beam, its loss was not really a serious inconvenience: on a ketch we could sail well enough on the big genoa and the mizzen, still a well-balanced rig.

The wind rose to Force 6–7 one night, but it was short lived; the Azores High, which had been moving up towards Newfoundland at the start of the voyage now chose instead to stretch right across from the Azores to the UK. So it was all sail down and the last three days were spent motoring, again. Murmurings were heard from the younger members of the crew when I suggested we make the most of what wind there was, on the grounds that this was meant to be a sailing boat, but I was overruled. Probably a wise decision: first Ireland to the south and then Islay ahead soon hove into sight.

We put in to Port Ellen on Islay partly because the pilot book told us we could clear customs there (only to learn that the office had been closed for four years) and partly because Dorothy, Alastair's wife, had come out here to meet us. Frank chose this moment to leave us and caught the ferry to the mainland; it was apparently something to do with internal family politics. I thanked him for his company and for his help, and meant it genuinely.

In Port Ellen we disentangled the mainsail from the two halves of the boom, carried it on to the quayside, and carefully folded and stowed it away. After renewing some stores we motored across the Sound of Jura and on towards Loch Sween and so to Tayvallich, where the owner had a mooring. We arrived amid great excitement and a big family welcome for the owner and his brother, after their first Atlantic crossing, and in their 'new' boat.

Maybe it wasn't my favourite Atlantic crossing, but it was certainly not without incident.

A PACIFIC VENTURE

If you can make one heap of all your winnings,
And risk it on one turn of pitch and toss,
And lose, and start again at your beginnings...
IF, RUDYARD KIPLING

From the Atlantic to the Pacific. After losing *Dodo's Delight* to fire in 2005 I replaced her with another Westerly 33 Discus and transferred the name. The new boat had some osmosis in her hull laminate, which was perhaps too radically peeled by a boatyard I had taken it to in Scotland, whether through their fault or mine remains debatable. But this did at least allow for two layers of epoxy resin to be applied. In spite of the extra expense I hoped this would strengthen the hull for future expeditions. Altogether I spent three years or so refurbishing the boat, including some personal modifications such as leading all the control and reefing lines back to the cockpit. Then in the winter of 2008/9 my son David made a solid sprayhood or cuddy, just as he had done for the first *Dodo*; on both boats it has been a tremendous boon.

Work on the new *Dodo* continued unabated until 2008 and was costing more than I could raise from ski instructing and from using the boat whenever possible for my charity at the time, Enterprise Sailing. Therefore it was a great help when an American sailing friend, Scott, kindly offered to give a donation in return for my assisting him sail his boat from Costa Rica to Alaska, via Hawaii.

I had met Scott the year before. David and Judy (Royal Cruising Club friends) had sailed their boat *Cloud Walker* to Murmansk in Russia, but David became ill on the return passage and was admitted to hospital at Kirkenes in the far north-east of Norway. Scott and I went out and helped Judy sail the boat back round the North Cape to Trømso.

To a Brit the name of Scott's boat resonated with pleasing historical overtones. Billy Ruffian had been the sailors' name for the *Bellepheron*, a 74-gun third-rate ship of the line in Nelson's navy, present at Trafalgar. Napoleon had also made his final surrender on her after Waterloo. This present-day *Billy Ruff'n* was a 47-foot steel Van de Stadt-designed Samoa three-quarter rigged sloop. It had all the appearance of being a powerful boat, given wind. But therein lay the rub.

Costa Rica to Hawaiian Islands

There were three of us aboard for this first passage: Scott, the 'gentle American' owner and skipper, Tom, an American doctor recently returned from a medical assignment in Chile, and myself. I flew from Scotland to Orlando, Florida, where I met Scott, fresh from a rafting holiday. We then flew in a small piston-engine plane all too reminiscent of the terrors of past parachuting for my liking, and arrived at Golfito, Costa Rica. Coming from the deep snows of Bavaria, where I had been teaching army groups skiing and ski mountaineering, the heat of Golfito was extreme and enervating. We sought relief in the shade of the local bar over an ice-cold beer or two in between loading stores, diesel and water to the very brim. Tom had arrived by now, but before departure we took the boat to the other side of the bay where Scott dived under in full diving kit to give the bottom a good scrub before we motored out into the Pacific.

We knew this was going to be a long and windless passage, at least for the first part. It soon became obvious that it was going to be different for me in other ways, too. For a start, all these American boats seemed to want to keep in touch with each other via the Ham radio network. Part of this radio traffic comprised of a general injunction to report one's position and course, the wind direction, wind strength and numerous other details, daily, to some controller on land.

I could not help wondering what had happened to the peace and solitude of ocean sailing, and the mantra 'On mountains and sea/If ye canna look after yourself/There you should not be,' came to mind. I did not see why someone miles away on land should tell me what the weather was like where I was and direct which way I should go, however well meaning and well informed they might be. An over-reaction, perhaps, but I had just come from giving the weather lecture to soldiers on a course in Bavaria, which I usually concluded by saying: 'Study the clouds, watch the barometer, and spoil yourself by learning to read a synoptic chart, and you will know the weather.' The contrast was glaring.

For the first 1400 miles we sailed when we could and motored when we could not, which was most of the time. There were some high points. I loved the fact that at these latitudes you could see the Southern Cross to the south slowly turning on itself, and at the same time the North Star to the north, with the Big Dipper wheeling around it. And whereas in the Atlantic fulmars and gannets skim around the boat, and petrels and albatrosses (B52s, my crew used to call them) in the far south, here we were apparently accompanied only by shearwaters, usually of the sooty variety. In these waters, too, there were plenty of dolphins, some of whom appeared to have perfected the back flip.

And low points. Our own Black Monday: the day after Scott had manfully rigged the servo-pendulum rudder on the Aries self-steering system by hanging over the stern on a line, while we were motoring through the night a bolt had fallen out, and the force of the water had bent the shaft of the rudder. The Aries would not now hold a course. Then, first one and then the other electronic autopilot gave up the ghost, so we were forced to hand-steer for a while until we managed to resuscitate the main one the next day, or so we thought.

At last the Trade winds kicked in – although we were not allowed to call them the Trades until we had reached 140°W where our routing charts said they officially began. Soon I was reminded of the downside to Trade-wind sailing: the continuous rolling from side to side that goes with it. And were these the Trade winds anyway? Where were the nice fluffy, white cumulus clouds? At least there was wind, and the 'Trades' bowled us along for a few days before they too died away to nothing. By then the autopilot had died once more, so the three of us spent the next 2300 miles of the passage hand-steering day and night – watch-on, watch-off, sailing or motoring. It became something of an endurance test.

The next thing to die was the computer, which meant no electronic charts or weather faxes from now on. This was a blow, at least as far as Scott was concerned. I felt sorry for him; he had spent an immense amount of time and effort, and probably money, preparing the boat. We tried to assure him that most ocean sailors navigated by GPS and paper charts anyway, rather than chartplotters on an empty ocean.

There was some cheer for the crew, as they had politely excused me from cooking duty. It suited me, there being no porridge or haggis on board, or even good old American corned beef. I became expert at washing up instead.

Other omissions could have been more serious. On one occasion, distracted by what was going on at the bows, when the big lightweight foresail drifter was being taken down, our 'more experienced ocean sailor' (me) inadvertently let the boom gybe across. Thankfully the preventer was rigged and the boom did not come crashing fully over. On another, when we needed to heave-to for repairs, confidently shouting 'gybe-oh', I promptly tacked the boat through the wind, instead of turning the wheel the other way and gybing as I'd said. But kindly some time later the crew baked a cake to mark my 'first 100,000 miles' at sea, with 100 written on it, which they were at pains to suggest had nothing to do with my age but only the mileage.

Scott was now getting weather information by satellite phone from an agency called Commanders on the American mainland. But the information did not seem to bear a great deal of resemblance to what we were actually experiencing. We jilled around at their behest, first to the south and then to the north, looking for wind, but finally decided, with Scott's agreement, that for a small boat on a huge ocean this was a fruitless exercise. Fortunately the Trade winds finally returned and settled in, and for the last few days constant north-easterlies pushed us forcefully towards Hawaii.

This gave Tom, with his sail racing experience, the opportunity to coach us in the finer points of sail tuning, which was probably no bad thing. Through no fault of his the drifter suddenly burst one day and collapsed into the sea. It was quite an effort hauling this huge sail out of the water and laying it along the side deck to dry out. However we were at last making progress, and we even had two days of white fluffy clouds, sunshine, and a continual blessed wind.

By this time, the passage having taken longer than expected, Tom was getting behind schedule and anxious, so we diverted to make our landfall at Hilo on the island of Hawaii, rather than going direct to Honolulu. This island has a high active volcanic mountain in its midst, indicative of how the whole chain had been formed by volcanoes erupting from the sea bed. The volcano was completely hidden in cloud all the time we were approaching and so of no navigational help to us, but with GPS it wasn't a problem: we just went from one waypoint to another into harbour. It had been 4500 miles in thirty-one days, only marred by a lack of wind and having to hand-steer for such a long way.

Honolulu

Having dropped Tom off, a day or two later Scott and I sailed the boat on to Honolulu. This required tricky pilotage through the islands, with some strong tidal streams to contend with. Honolulu came as a shock – tall modern shiny structures punctuated the entire skyline. I suppose I had unconsciously expected some sort of quaint Hawaiian architecture rather than what I now realised was really an American city. Once through the narrow harbour entrance we tied up alongside at the yacht club.

No sooner had we made fast than Scott was on the phone to a friend, and that very evening we found ourselves having dinner and staying the night at the elegant house of a four-star American admiral, the former Commander-in-Chief of the US Pacific fleet no less, and his wife. He and Scott had been shipmates in Scott's naval days. They were delightful people and it was a wonderful evening and sleepover, especially after thirty-one days at sea.

We spent over two weeks in Honolulu, busily maintaining the boat. And before we knew it the time had flown and we needed to go to the airport to pick up new crew.

To Alaska and beyond

We still had another 2500 miles to go to Alaska. For this passage we were to be joined by Mike and his partner Heather. Mike was British, but manager of a heli-ski operation in Canada, and Heather was also involved in the Canadian ski industry. At the airport I looked around for them at eye level as one does, to be greeted at last by Mike recumbent on an airport bench just below. I assumed he was resting from the flight. Introductions were made and we drove back to the boat. It transpired later that Mike was suffering from back trouble, which was to plague him throughout the trip.

Heather had expressed a wish to do all the cooking, and who could complain at that? Not that we had eaten badly so far (Scott and Tom had done brilliantly on the previous passage) but things were clearly set to look up even more. We would be well fed. Mike, as well as leaping about as the self-appointed deckhand in spite of his bad back, took on the role of ship's photographer and tried to educate me in modern technology. The digital camera he had cleverly persuaded me to buy in Honolulu had somehow become the ship's camera.

After a day or two it became clear that a lack of wind would not be among our problems. We were able to sail almost the whole way, and indeed enjoyed some fine sailing days and nights. After some attention in Honolulu the Aries chose to work, but I found it hard work reefing the mainsail. The boat was fitted with slab reefing, which meant whole sections of the sail could be hauled down to the boom as the wind strength increased. Scott had a reliable method of doing this, but it meant going up to the mast and lowering the mainsail until a steel ring in the luff or front of the sail could be slipped onto a hook at the fore part of the boom. So far so good, but then it required winding down whichever was the correct coloured rope for the required slab reef using a big winch at the mast under the boom, to bring the leech or aft end of the sail down to the boom. It was heavy work: this was a big but surprisingly spritely boat under sail, and the gear was accordingly heavy.

We were sailing fast now, in fairly big seas, but often in sunshine. Heather at this stage was beginning to regret her offer to do all the cooking, and understandably so in such lively conditions.

We found ourselves one evening in thick fog and I was rather surprised when Scott asked us to make a Securité call every half hour on the VHF radio, giving our position, course and speed, in case there were other boats in the vicinity. Scott and I obviously had rather different attitudes regarding sailing and safety. After all, I thought, we had a powerful radar which would show any ships up to a range of 16 miles.

It was even more surprising when, spotting a deep depression 200–250 miles ahead on the weather fax on the repaired computer, we hove-to for 10 hours in spite of a nice sailing breeze, in case we caught up with it. Then 12 hours before another predicted gale we rigged the storm trysail in place of the mainsail, quite an exacting operation in its own right. In the event the wind did pick up to 30–35 knots the next day. As reefing was heavy work it made sense to do it at some stage, but it did seem rather premature. We might have done things rather differently, but you cannot have two skippers on a boat, and we sailed as friends and finished as friends, and that was the important thing.

A fine passage was only slightly spoilt by having to motor for most of the last three days when the wind gave out. Inevitably, in spite of the highly expensive replacements effected in Honolulu, the autopilot also chose this moment to fail and, under motor, we were back to hand-steering again. But we passed through some stunning scenery as we approached the coast of Alaska with its many heavily forested small islands, eventually putting in to the town of Seward. Safely berthed in a small space alongside a pontoon, we broke open the Scotch and toasted our passage.

Alaska

We spent several days in Seward. Scott found a café where we could connect to the internet and send emails. We ate out occasionally at an excellent harbour-front café, with seafood of course; I took Scott out to dinner on one occasion to thank him, which seemed to be appreciated, and some evenings Mike and Heather went off clubbing. Apart from looking around the town, we set to work on the boat.

This was a smart, well maintained 47-foot boat. Being steel, however, any rust had to be dealt with radically and immediately. It had been spray-painted white, including the decks, which meant any scuffs or even tread marks showed up. In harbour we were set to scrubbing – and scrubbing. Scott was fanatical; he even scrubbed where we had just scrubbed (which may not have said much for our efforts). The boat was shining by the time his wife, Svea, joined us (ah, had that been the reason?). Svea said she was also keen on cooking, and I wondered how the girls would work that one out. Scott and myself were only too happy to encourage them of course.

Scrubbed and gleaming, our boat hugged the coast of Alaska. I believe it has the highest coastal mountain range in the world, and it was beautiful. Prince William Sound was a magical place with sea, hills and forests all around. We saw black bears on the shoreline and approached fairly close in the dinghy to photograph them. From there we headed for Icy Bay with its glacier, growlers and brash calving off and floating in the water. Having had some experience with ice I was entrusted to steer. A steel boat is safer in ice compared to a glassfibre boat, and *Billy Ruff'n* was easily able to push her way through without damage. From the dinghy we took photographs of the fine sight of the boat surrounded by ice, and later Mike stripped off and went swimming in the icy water. We took a photo of him standing up with only a lump of brash ice preserving his modesty.

We continued eastwards along this lovely coastline, with its mountains and glaciers coming right down to the sea, and found a wide indent, also called Icy Bay. We went in to get a better view of Mount St Elias. At just over 18,000 feet this is the second highest mountain in Alaska, and on the North American continent. It was certainly impressive and doubly so for me. We were anchored underneath the peak and from the vantage point of the boat I couldn't resist trying to work out possible routes up it. The bay was well named: it was beset by ice. We played around, driving the boat up very close to a large bergy bit until the skipper wisely called a halt. To starboard, a fjord that the chart suggested was filled with a glacier was in fact now open water. Whatever the reasons may be for climate change, the glaciers here had definitely receded.

We made our way further down the coast to the system of fjords and islands that lead in to Juneau, and set to with more boat scrubbing so we could leave it clean and tidy. Then came the farewells: time for Mike, Heather and me to express our considerable thanks for a great trip. Mike and Heather made their way home to the mountains of Canada, and I, through Scott's generosity in routing my flights that way, was able to spend a few days with our son Peter in San Francisco, before flying on from there to Scotland.

It had been 8004 miles from Costa Rica to Juneau – a sailing marathon, but what an enjoyable one.

BILLY BUDD

*And it may be that he liked this adventurous turn in his affairs which
promised an opening into novel scenes and martial excitements.*
BILLY BUDD, HERMAN MELVILLE

From San Francisco I flew back to Scotland and two days later, with
hardly enough time to wash my clothes in between, I flew out to
Greenland as 'Arctic Adviser' on a 56-foot yacht, or so I thought.

The 56-footer turned out to be a 72-foot Oyster Marine yacht,
Billy Budd – only the third one they had built. With a sleek shining
hull and fitted with every comfort, including a huge Refleks diesel
heater, it promised to be another novel experience: a true superyacht,
as different from *Dodo* as it could be. Richard Haworth's company
High Latitudes had advised Mariacristina (Cristina) and Giovanni
(*Billy Budd*'s Italian owners) during the construction and fitting out
of the boat, and he was our skipper for this voyage. There was also an
engineer (Luca), deckhand (Richard, but known as 'Young Richard'
to distinguish him from the skipper) and cook/mate (Kali). Life
aboard would bear no resemblance to what I was accustomed to, nor
would the process of getting there. On previous trips, Copenhagen
airport had often found me sleeping on an airport bench for reasons
of economy. On the last occasion I had told myself, 'never again at
your age', and this time I was put up at the adjacent Hilton Hotel.
That evening Cristina and Giovanni summoned me from my room
and introduced me to their friends, Luca (not the engineer) and Daria,
who were coming as guests, and Gianni, an Alpine mountain guide
hired for the summer. Next morning we all flew on to Greenland
in grand style; Cristina had changed all our tickets to business class:
another first for me.

This was flying as I had never experienced it, and it quickly became
a case of 'enjoy it while you can'. The flight attendants slid gracefully
down the wide aisles between the plush seats and like a schoolboy
on a day out I accepted everything on offer. After changing at

Kangerlussuaq, the hub for nearly all onward flights in Greenland, we arrived replete (and perhaps slightly tipsy) at Aasiaat.

As Adviser, one of my jobs was to recommend anchorages on the way up the west coast of Greenland. Most of these suggestions were well received by the owners, as long as we were at anchor each evening by 1800 – so that cocktails could be served, followed by dinner in the saloon round the table, properly set with the saloon cushions plumped up (I was continually in trouble for forgetting to pat up the cushions). I did think that all too soon one could become accustomed to this way of life.

Cristina was as sharp as a needle, with a constantly enquiring mind, clearly a brilliant and successful patent lawyer, but also *simpatico*, generous and forgiving, just as long as you answered her questions speedily, rapier thrust to rapier thrust. Around about my second day on board came the question, 'So what are the five intellectual proofs for God?' Well, for more than forty years I had been ministering to young people, often intelligent and certainly canny, but not necessarily of great intellectual depth. Suffice it to say there had not been much call for the intellectual proofs for God in the East End of London or as chaplain to two slightly specialist schools; I could hardly remember their names, let alone how to spell some of them – ontological, epistemological, causal and so on. I certainly could not trot them out in an ordered manner. Then I lost more marks when Richard, the twenty-one-year-old deckhand, looked them up on Wikipedia.

I did regain some points later in the trip. It happened to be a Sunday, and I had dived on the wreck of my boat, the old *Dodo* sunk in a Greenland fjord. Someone asked Cristina later, 'An old priest on board? Did he say Mass?' 'No, he dived on the wreck of his boat,' she proudly replied. (Some have queried whether as a minister, or priest, I should be doing these sorts of things. But I see no discrepancy here. For a start, such activities made for excellent relationships with members of those youth clubs and boys at the school, and were a pleasing background and link to the pastoral work. And then, as Cliff

Richards quoted when his lifestyle was questioned, 'Why should the Devil have all the good music?' By the same token, why should a Reverend not also be an adventurer?)

From Aasiaat you have two alternatives when going north: round the west side of Disko Island, or eastwards through the Vaigat Channel, between Disko and the Nuussuaq peninsula, which is part of the mainland to the north. We went both ways: up the west side of Disko Island, which nowadays we should call Qeqertarsuaq, and then swapped over to the south and east. There was a reason for this: Luca, the guest, was a keen fly fisherman and it was rumoured that good fishing could be found in a certain fjord on the west side of Disko. Making our way across Disko Bay, with its icebergs calved from the huge Ilulissat glacier to the east, we put into Disko Fjord.

The anchorage described in the pilot book did not look either attractive or particularly secure, so we went farther in and found good shelter near the top of a subsidiary fjord, in good time for cocktails and dinner. But first, Luca and Young Richard went ashore. They fished hard but caught nothing. Finally, and I quote from the log, 'after a fruitless four hours the young deckhand put down his rod and scooped four Arctic char out of the river with his hands.' Luca's reaction is not recorded, but we ate well that night.

Next day we went south again, this time to Fortune Bay, a well protected, landlocked anchorage with just a keyhole entrance – Rich liked to play safe with someone else's boat. Our stay was rather spoilt that evening by clouds of midges, which can be just as aggravating on the west coast of Greenland as on the west coast of Scotland. We then crossed Disko Bay to Ilulissat in order to get a close-up look at the biggest glacier on the west coast of Greenland. On the way we clattered into a fair sized piece of ice when I was on watch, earning me a very disapproving look from the skipper.

First we viewed the glacier from seaward, but at a safe distance: bergs suddenly calving into the sea or shedding great lumps of ice have been known to kill locals fishing too close in their boats here.

Then we put in to Ilulissat harbour and a party walked across and viewed the glacier from a safer landward vantage point. Leaving the harbour later, crowded with local dories and fishing boats, where we had only just managed to find a place to moor, we passed a 180-foot ketch making its way in. We waved – it was rare to see another sailing boat in Greenland – but we did wonder where they were going to find even a square foot to moor.

In the Vaigat to the north, with its snow-capped mountains on either side, things began to get interesting: the wind increased and hit a steady 40 knots. Big icebergs abounded. 'We'll put in the fourth line of reefs, because I have never put them in before on this boat', said the skipper. We then rolled out the narrow blade inner staysail in place of the bigger foresail, and continued to pick our way carefully through the icebergs. This was more like the Greenlandic sailing we were used to. That evening I guided them in to Atanikerdluk on the northern shore of the Vaigat, with its sheltered bays either side of a peninsula, providing protection whatever the wind direction. I was secretly pleased about this as I had 'found' these anchorages in a previous year and written them up for the *Faroes, Iceland and Greenland Pilot*, edited by Willy Ker.

In Atanikerdluk we came across a French boat, a 45-foot steel Ovni, and made contact on the VHF. They were also going north so it was the same the following night at the Nuussuaq anchorage at the far end of the Vaigat. Here, we signed the visitors' book at the *rejsehus* (a hut used on the old winter sledding route) and visited an old Norse stone ruin called *Bjornefælde*, which means bear trap, but is described in the pilot book as 'a small chapel used by the Norse settlers during the summer hunt... dating from the thirteenth century.' I have never been sure how those two marry up.

The Ovni came in and anchored close by, and I went across in the dinghy to have a blether, as we say in Scotland, and was rather pleased to find a copy of Willy Ker's pilot book on their chart table with a cover photo of the old *Dodo*, taken through the arch of an iceberg.

What vanity! Some of our shore party made their way round the head of the bay to the old trading station, probably built in the early twentieth century. The main building was still more or less intact, as were the foundations of the adjoining dwellings. The nearby cemetery witnessed the usual sad reminder of the early death of children in the past in this land.

Crossing the wide open Uummannaq Fjord we motored round to the east side of the large island of Upernavik Ø (Ø means island in Danish) to the fjord that separates it from the mainland and makes it an island. The shores were steep-to and we had some difficulty finding a place to anchor, but before long we found a suitable depth on a silt bank where a mountain stream flowed into the fjord.

The next day a number of us went across to Upernavik Ø in the large rigid inflatable kept on the spacious foredeck, to climb an attractive peak on the island. Kali and I set off first, followed by the others. All the rest except Gianni and Kali turned back after a while, leaving us to continue together up the increasingly steep and bouldery slope. This then turned into a scramble up rock steps near the top where Gianni threw us down a rope, which was just as well as the rubber of my cheap boots did not take kindly to the wet rock. An attractive peak it may have been, but it was a long way. We made it to the top to find a small tin in a cairn with a note in it stating that a party from St Andrew's University had climbed the peak in 1984. St Andrew's used to keep a house on Uberkendt Island the other side of Upernavik Ø, ostensibly for geological purposes, but they seemed also to have fitted in a fair amount of climbing.

We descended by a different route. By this time I was suffering again with a recurrence of Tilman's 'Mountaineer's Foot'. Kali, the young gazelle, and Gianni, the Alpine mountain guide, were down long before me, but kindly made no comment.

We meandered up the west coast of Greenland, round the Svartenhuk peninsula fringed by its usual huge collection of icebergs, and so on to the settlement of Kangersuartsiaq (Prøven). The approach from the south is by a narrow channel where the depth has to be watched closely. *Billy Budd* had to anchor outside the main harbour bay to stay clear of the reefs and shallows within.

Kangersuartsiaq is probably the most picturesque settlement in Greenland, so it was worth spending the time and energy to climb the hill above to take pictures of the town with its background of fjord, bergs and mountains. Behind the town we discovered some low rock cliffs which gave some excellent bouldering and rock-climbing practice. Kali had done little climbing before so we took a rope and soon the tutored was outstripping the tutor.

As we made our way northwards through the fjords, the mountains became even more dramatic. One of my other duties was to find rock climbs for Cristina and Gianni, so I took them round to the Sortehul channel, a fjord some twenty miles south-east of Upernavik (the town, no connection with the island 150 miles to the south). We were anchored by a pleasant beach at the southern end of the Sortehul with another *rejsehus* nearby, and Cristina and Gianni went off to a cliff which looked as if it could be climbed in a day – most of the climbing here involves a seriously long day or even several days. They returned in the evening well pleased. It had not been a particularly hard climb, but it was the first route on a new cliff.

Upernavik and the North

It was on the way round to Upernavik when Cristina and Giovanni allowed me time to dive on the wreck of *Dodo's Delight*. It was a salutary experience. Nothing but the bare shell, like an open rowing boat, was left down there. Fire, ice and storm seemed to have stripped her bare; I came to the surface holding only the mangled remains of my old Arctic sleeping bag. At least that chapter was now fully closed.

We made a brief stop in Upernavik for stores and diesel, and I renewed acquaintance with friends from my winter months previously. Peter (and his Inuit friend with an unpronounceable name) had shown me how they hunted seals in the winter, using a net cunningly laid out under the ice by using a tuk, and after the fire they had taken me back on their skidoo to the site to rescue the tent I had left ashore. I also bought a *tuk* for the boat: a wooden pole with a metal blade at the end, used by Greenlanders for testing the ice when they are walking across it in the winter, but also useful to us for pushing blocks of ice away from the boat.

From Upernavik we sailed the 150 miles or so north to the Tommelfinger, better known as 'The Devil's Thumb', a 300-metre prominent finger of rock which Cristina wanted to climb with Gianni. They invited me along.

'Are you sure you are not too old for this sort of thing, Cristina?' I said jocularly, deliberately forgetting that I was at least twenty years older than her.

'Are you sure a priest should be climbing this?' came the immediate reply – it was after all called 'The Devil's Thumb'. Touché!

It was a grand climb, a long prominent crack line on its big south face, with the difficulties increasing gradually the farther up we went. For someone who had not been climbing seriously for a long time, it was a help that the crux pitches were near the top and I could warm up on the easier pitches lower down. At the top we phoned the boat on the handheld VHF to let them know all was well. As we looked around, the view was magnificent, the ice-filled fjord below with the boat, looking tiny there at anchor, and stretching away to mountains and the inland ice cap. But getting back down was not too easy, involving several abseil pitches and trusting that Gianni had made secure anchorages for the rope each time. We could not claim it as a first ascent, but we wondered whether it was the first female ascent, and I tentatively claimed it as the oldest person's ascent.

The coastline curves round to the west at the top of Melville Bay. Cape York was surprisingly free of icebergs, unusual in my experience. We put in to Parker Snow Bugt (names in Greenland are often evocative), a pleasant, sheltered bay open only to the south and with a curious uniformly triangular rocky hill at its head. We could only think this had been formed by the terminal moraines of two glaciers meeting, and which had now receded. Or it might have been an ancient pingo. Farther on we came across the wide Pituffik glacier and Giovanni, Gianni, Kali and Young Richard piled in to the RIB to take photos of the boat silhouetted against the long glacier face. A huge ice shelf had broken off the north-western corner of the glacier since I was here last, completely negating the shelter it might have afforded to the anchorage recorded in the pilot book. Historically there was an added piquancy to this. Elisha Kent Kane's *Advance* had been trapped in ice for two winters in Rensselaer Bay at 79°N in Nares Strait. When he and the survivors finally abandoned ship in their desperation and made their way south in two rowing boats, they had stopped here in 1855 and eaten the dovekies (little auks) and their eggs in the cave in the cliff above. They would have been hard put to do it now with all the growlers and bergy bits in the new inlet by the cave.

That evening we made our way rather cautiously into North Star Bay, named after James Saunders's expedition aboard *North Star*, which was marooned in the bay from 1849–1850, and now the site of the massive US Armed Forces' Thule Air Base. Yachts of any sort, even American, have not been welcome in the past, but we were told by radio that as long as we kept to the head of the bay and did not try to enter the base that would be OK. We did go ashore but only to walk round to the west to view the old Inuit settlement of Thule, displaced by the American 'invasion' of 1951. It is difficult to be objective about this, as the story goes that the Inuit population woke up one morning to find American ships and landing craft unannounced and unloading tons of equipment to build and set up their new air base. The Americans had worked out a secret deal with the Danish government, but it appears nobody had told the local inhabitants, who were then told to look for another site. They finally settled on the site now known variously and rather confusingly as Thule or Qaanaaq, some 100 miles to the north of the original Thule.

Little of the original settlement was left standing, but what was there was of considerable interest. As I had seen before, the walls of the houses were of turf interlaced with flat stones for stability, and the insides were lined with a wooden structure. The inhabitants would have been both warm and relatively comfortable inside, the turf walls and roof providing tremendous protection from the elements, and the lining giving comfort and extra insulation from the cold. The Inuit have always been streaks ahead of Europeans when it comes to survival in the Arctic, a lesson the Norse who settled here for 400 years at the southern end of Greenland never really learned. They might have survived longer if they had.

On the way westwards we stopped at Moriusaq, a small settlement beloved of Sir Wally Herbert. Wally Herbert had been knighted for his extraordinary achievements in Arctic exploration, albeit rather belatedly on account, it is generally assumed, of some frank communiqués he had sent from near the North Pole to his committee back home during his traverse over the top of the world. He had always been enthusiastic about this settlement, the closest survivor of an ancient hunting culture, he claimed. But we found it virtually deserted, and with few husky dogs to be seen. Eventually we came across a local couple who told us (with some language difficulty) that there were now only eleven inhabitants left living in the settlement. One wondered how long it would survive.

Arctic Canada

Cristina and Giovanni had decided we would not go farther north to Qaanaaq and beyond, so we set a course for Canada, putting in first to Bethune Inlet on the east side of the huge Devon Island, curious to see where the British whaler *Queen* had wintered in 1866/7. We anchored in Queen Bay, took a transit on to some rocks on the shore, and … they moved; the rocks turned out to be a colony of well-disguised walrus. We went ashore and were amused at their antics, huffing and puffing, and diving in to swim, play and hunt. Giovanni and party also came across four musk oxen standing solitary in a snow field to the north. Lugubriously forming a defensive circle, they in their turn surveyed these strange creatures looking at them. Near the shore we stumbled upon the foundations of four ancient Inuit turf houses, and wondered whether they had been inhabited when the *Queen* had overwintered here. It was a fantastic place.

A day or two later we went over to the other side of the fjord and anchored at its southern end, where land appeared again abutting the huge glacier. A well-equipped party led by Gianni went for a short exploration of the glacier and its streams. That evening with everyone back on board, a polar bear left the shore and swam slowly around the boat looking to see what this strange black 'whale' was doing in its territory. The rifle was fetched just in case, but we were spellbound. And as if that was not enough, in the night, but with full daylight in the Arctic, another polar bear came to visit, this time on its back with a cub sitting on its chest for safety and warmth.

Elated by these sights we fetched our anchor next morning and motored down the coast of Devon Island, into Lancaster Sound and across to Navy Board Inlet, the channel on the west side of Bylot Island. So many names in the Arctic are British, but Navy Board Inlet does seem to be scraping the barrel.

Near Tay Bay on the Bylot Island side another polar bear came to the shore to have a look at us. Tay Bay was where an American, Alvah Simon, had wintered alone in his boat. He wrote a successful book about it, *North to the Night*, which I am afraid I found rather over dramatic. Farther south we entered an area of fjords, cliffs and mountains some forty miles south-west of the settlement of Pond Inlet. We took in a climb as a taster, naming the new route *Lasagne or Porridge*. We had eaten Italian lasagne at supper the night before, and the team could never get over my insistence on having Scottish porridge for breakfast.

That evening we were visited by a boat-load of Greenlanders out on a weekend family camping and hunting trip, stocking up for a winter that would be upon them all too soon. They seemed fascinated by this large yacht and what it was doing in 'their' fjord, and we were intrigued by their open canoe with its outboard motor and inquisitive human cargo (replete with kids). Pond Inlet on Baffin Island was and to an extent still is Canadian so they had a smattering of English, although we knew no Inuit. All too soon they waved a warm farewell and sped off home towards Pond Inlet.

Getting to Pond Inlet next morning seemed to take a long time. There was so much to see: the glacier to the north on Bylot Island that Polly and Tashy had come down at the end of their traverse in 2001; the Sermilik glacier a little farther on that Maxi and I had also come down a few days later. Rich, the skipper, had forgotten all about the fact that I had been there as well as Polly, which put me in my place.

Our time was coming to an end; Luca, Daria, Gianni, and myself were about to return home. Cristina and Giovanni came to the airport to see us off, and we said our sad goodbyes before catching the flight home. But it was not to be by business class this time.*

---

* A pleasing footnote to *Billy Budd*'s trip was that Rich and Cristina were awarded the Tilman Medal for the expedition. This was in large part due to their achievements on the subsequent leg, when they went halfway down the east coast of Baffin Island, making some notable first ascents of rock climbs on the way. They also saw numerous polar bears, so the poor mountain guide had to carry a rifle on his back up extreme rock climbs.

07

ARCTIC ANTICS

To dare is to lose one's footing momentarily. Not to dare is to lose oneself.

SOREN KIERKEGAARD

If you were to ask me, 'What is this fascination with the Arctic? Why do you keep going back there?' I would be hard put to give you an answer. After all, it is desolate, remote, glacial, icebound, cold and treeless. But maybe that is the attraction; the very desolation, the unrelenting nature of the land and sea. And of course there is the added challenge of first ascents. In short, as many who go there will attest, the Arctic and Antarctic are addictive. So what a joy to return to the Arctic once more for a proper adventure.

PARADISE REGAINED – OR AT LEAST REVISITED

I had spent some three to four years refurbishing the replacement for my first *Dodo's Delight*, and had taken her on a warm-up, shake-down cruise to the Azores and back in 2008. Now at last we could think of revisiting Paradise: it was time to return to Greenland, do some climbing and, also, to set up an automatic weather station on Littleton Island for The Scottish Association for Marine Science (SAMS) and the Danish Space Agency.

'That meanest Atlantic crossing of them all', from Scotland to Greenland, lived up to its billing – a tough passage, but not necessarily for the usual stormy reasons. For a start we were shorthanded. The experienced mate I was relying on had rolled her car a few weeks before and perhaps unwisely decided that a sea voyage would prove she had regained rude health. So she was surprised when heaving up the anchor at St Kilda on someone else's boat that 'something went' in her back. We were down to three. Then during the passage, the newly promoted mate, whom we will call Martin, told me he had recently been diagnosed with Asperger's syndrome. This explained his rather off-putting lack of response on some occasions. Had my instructions, suggestions or information been received, accepted or even heard? A modus vivendi was however established, punctuated by the occasional flare-up. And although not a qualified mountaineer, he was strong, fit and competent on mountains, and he was an experienced and skilful sailor, even if he liked to have things done the one way. The other member of the crew was Vicki, who had become a friend during our years as fellow ski instructors in Bavaria. Comparatively inexperienced as a sailor she may have been, but she was gutsy, keen, capable and quick to learn.

So we wended our way up the Sound of Mull, and anchored overnight in the well-protected Loch Drumbuie by Tobermory. Next day it was across the Minch to anchor for the night by the airstrip on Barra, which is famously on the beach. The Sound of Barra led out from the Outer Hebrides, by now my favoured departure point into the Atlantic. The second day out the eye of the halyard at the head of the genoa burst. I was glad of the steps that I had recently had fitted to the mast to reach the truck, but it took me some time sitting in a climbing harness at the top of the mast to rig a jury halyard.

Fortunately it was calm that day, and the temporary repair proved successful, but the rolling in the wider arc you get from side to side at the masthead left me feeling sick for twenty-four hours afterwards.

It was two hours on, four hours off, watch-on, watch-off without a break across the North Atlantic, and the windvane self-steering chose not to work most of the time, so we were hand-steering nearly all the way. Those more used to offshore rather than ocean sailing are often surprised to be told there is no need to sail a direct course towards the destination when the wind is against you. It just stresses boat and crew. Much better to close reach on the making tack, as Geoff Hales had counselled years before. After all, our next waypoint was 1200 miles away on the other side of the Atlantic, simply a rough cross on the chart to make sure we kept well clear of Cape Farewell at the southern tip of Greenland.

We hove-to or lay a-hull three times, due to strong wind and sea as you would expect, but also when there was no wind at all to save wear and tear on the sails slatting back and forth in the swell. In the end the wind direction pushed us closer to Cape Farewell than our intended 150 miles to the south. But the winds were now light again and the weather fine, and there, 70 miles to starboard, were 'Greenland's icy mountains', as the hymn has it. We were accompanied by whales, minke I think, breaching and blowing, sometimes a little too close for comfort.

Heading up the west coast of Greenland past Cape Desolation we encountered our first bergy bits and icebergs. The wind was quite strong by now and we were goosewinged much of the time. At first Vicki found it difficult to keep both sails filled and avoid the ice, but she soon got the hang of it. We passed a huge tabular iceberg where the wind increased noticeably on approach, and then some other big icebergs. We speculated about their glacial origin as we made our way northwards to Paamiut, our first port of call.

The morning found us hanging off our mooring warps, which once again we had left with insufficient slack, but at least I had remembered the lesson learned in Qaqortoq years before – no jamming hitches this time, so the warps were easy to untie. Fuelled and watered, we left Paamiut that same day. This was a mistake, as it took us straight out into a strong northerly and we had to tack across Davis Strait towards Baffin Island. I wondered whether a long dark smudge on the horizon could possibly be Baffin itself. In fact it was a fog bank which soon enveloped us. Next morning we put about on the other tack, but the wind eventually gave out and we had to resort to the engine, and put in to Sisimiut to top up fuel… and just as important, loo rolls!

Later, motoring out of Sisimiut, there, coming up the channel, was a small sailing boat. Could that possibly be… '*Assent, Assent*, this is *Dodo's Delight*'. '*Dodo's Delight*, this is *Assent*, how are you, Bob?' It was Willy Ker, the grand old master of Greenlandic sailing, and also editor of the RCC pilot book for the area. *Assent* came alongside and Willy came on board for a dram. 'So you have whisky on board?' 'Yes, Willy, it probably dates from when you were last on board.' Willy was in Aasiaat by the time we arrived there, and so were Cristina and Giovanni on *Billy Budd* and we were all invited to a slap-up dinner on their superyacht, which made three Tilman Medal-holders together. I met another, Arved Fuchs, on board *Dagmar Aalen* at Qaanaq later that year. It had clearly been a busy summer in the Arctic for explorers.

At Aasiaat Vicki had to leave us, and Thomas, an experienced sailor, joined us as the new mate. Then Tom, a climber and ski instructor, also flew out to join us. We made our way round the west side of Disko Island and then northwards across Uummannaq Fjord to Ingia Fjord and the Akuliarusinguaq peninsula. A mass of ice met us at the top of Ingia Fjord, and we were forced to lace a course through gaps and leads. Nilas, large sheets or floes of thin ice, blocked our way and on one occasion we had to rev the engine hard to break the sheet open to make any progress. Fortunately there was more open water on the other side of the fjord, and we were able to reach Puartdlarsivik and as in previous years drop our anchor on the silt fan stretching out from the glacial river.

I have occasionally seen icebergs roll over when they have become top-heavy, but at anchor here, fortunately not too close to us, a big one suddenly turned right over, but then continued to roll from side to side, see-sawing and making a huge roaring noise for several minutes, before it finally settled and quietened down in the water – a timely and rather frightening reminder, since we had recently been wending through the nearby ice, of the power of nature.

When it came to climbing – our main reason for being here – nothing seemed to go to plan. Our first ascent was thwarted. The glacier which should by a circuitous route have led us to our intended 2000-metre summit was guarded by a steep icefall. We, that is Tom, Thomas and I, did manage to climb it, using two axes and crampons each, but it just kept going on and on, pitch after pitch. I eventually reached the top, went a little farther, and looked along the glacier above. It did not look friendly; there in the distance was another system of crevasses or small icefalls awaiting us. It was obvious that with so few of us it was not going to be possible to carry camping and ski equipment up the icefalls and along what looked like a complicated glacier. We aborted the mission and returned to the boat, although this presented a challenge in itself: crossing the fast-flowing glacial rivers at the estuary. We reached the far shore soaked to the skin, and radioed Martin to come and fetch us.

The next mission, to climb two 2000-metre peaks at Nuugaatsiaup Tunua on the south side of the peninsula, was also unsuccessful, despite three days of strenuous effort attempting to do so. The three of us toiled over the boulder fields and up and across to the glacier, this time bivying rather uncomfortably in the rocks of the lateral moraine, higher up from where Gimlet and I had left our gear in 2004. Next morning, we continued up the snow shoulder that had cost me so dear – the snow was a little firmer this time – up the broken rocky bluff, and over *Solo Snow Dome* to the other side. But now came decision time. The 2000-metre peaks were in view, but time was getting on and there was still a long way to go over a well-defined ridge, which fell away particularly steeply on one side. We had run out of food, and to save weight had not brought gear for a brew. After a brief discussion we decided to call it a day. Tom did let slip that, had he been with younger men, he might have continued. But Thomas had already said he had reached his limit and was going down anyway, and I was tired enough to accept the decision and I was worried about our lack of sustenance. It was a long, weary plod back down, although Tom continued all the way to the bottom the same day – what it is to be young. Thomas and I bivied again among the boulders and descended the next day.

On a positive note, I was pleased to hear that Tom had found *Solo Snow Dome* to be 2090 metres and not 2060 as my rather unreliable altimeter had read previously. And before we decided to descend Tom had already taken in another subsidiary 2000-plus summit. It was not a completely wasted sortie. But overall we felt we had failed.

So what now? On the south-west corner of Akuliarusinguaq, Tom and Martin were much more successful, adding a classic cirque of unclimbed peaks in an area which none of us had visited before, one of which was a well-defined, good looking summit. Thomas and I, climbing separately next day, added more peaks. Coming down late off the final peak owing to the distances involved, I caused them concern. They could not see me against the background of the grassy slope as I crept slowly along after a very long day, and I was well overdue. But between us we had climbed ten virgin summits, so pride was satisfied, to some extent – the peaks were all part of the same long ridge line though there were ups and downs in between.

We moved on. A large number of big icebergs were there to be avoided as usual as we made our way along the southern shore of the Svartenhuk peninsula. About six miles from the settlement of Upernavik Kujalleq (formerly Sondre Upernavik) to the north, it looked as if we were about to run out of diesel, and I had visions of having to go there and back by dinghy in thick mist to collect fuel in a container, relying solely on GPS and VHF. But just then a soft breeze filled in from astern, and we were able to sail gently forward, only using the engine finally to reach the jetty and its welcoming diesel hose.

In the Sortehul region near Upernavik Tom and I enjoyed the first ascent of a 200-metre cliff in the sun, with the swell whispering seductively on the beach below, and on good rock. We called the climb *Old Man's Benefit*, for obvious reasons. Meantime, Thomas did his washing in a mountain stream below and manned the boat for us as, by his own admission, he was not a climber.

At Upernavik we met old friends. Further north the ice was thick round Cape York this time, and we sheltered for a night behind Wolstenholme Island in strong headwinds. Then, as thick mist enveloped the southern shore of Northumberland Island, we anchored off Upernavigssuaq, an abandoned Inuit settlement. I had fitted a chartplotter with radar to *Dodo* and it really came into its own here, approaching the coastline in this thick mist.

We had a day or two in hand before Andy was due to fly in and join the crew at Qaanaq, which gave us the chance to circumnavigate Northumberland Island identifying anchorages for the first ascents we were intending to make; it was time well spent. With Andy aboard we returned to Northumberland Island to climb. In brilliant style Tom and Andy, both experienced ski instructors, completed a technically difficult ski traverse of most of the length of the island, with steep descents and big crevasses, and which included six previously unclimbed summits. This is Tom's written account:

'We landed from the dinghy and crossed the terminal moraine to the glacier. We tried Harscheisen and skins on our skis but it was too difficult crossing the deep glacier streams and we swapped to crampons. After some 45 minutes of ascent we put skis and skins back on and roped up on the col for the ascent of Summit 1 (Pt 1030 metres). The descent from here looked fairly heavily crevassed, but we skied down a little more to the east. Excellent snow and a steep run, jumping some crevasses. Skins back on and a fairly straightforward ascent to Summit 2 (Pt 827 metres), then we continued the ski traverse avoiding (at this stage) Summit 3 to a bivy spot, but we were unable to pitch the tent due to steep snow and a large boulder field. In the end we bivied in the boulder field using the tent as a bivy bag. It was a splendid evening.

'Next day (21 August) we traversed to the col, left our packs and made a quick ascent of Summit 3 (Pt 930). We returned to our sacks and then had to make a horrendous crossing of a gravel boulder field carrying our skis on our backs to the glacier. Fog was descending as we commenced the ascent to Summit 4 (Pt 1000). Big crevasses here required anchors and belaying. One crevasse was jumped with skis off. It was all hard going. As we got out of the crevasse field the fog cleared but it was very windy. From Summit 4 we went on to Summit 5 (Pt 950) and then very rapid skinning on snow led to Summit 6 (another Pt 950). An initially tentative descent took us to a narrow, steep gully between gravel fields and glacier streams, but on good snow which was just as well.

'We hit the top of Sermiarssugssuaq glacier which gave a crevasse-jumping descent turning into Cairngorm skiing with ice, mud and "mogul" fields. The finish comprised a never-ending slog over the terminal moraine to pitch the tent on the sea shore. A good night's sleep was interrupted at 3 a.m. when Andy realised we were about to drown with the rising tide. Next morning the boat made its way through ice floes and picked us up.'

To add to the bag, the old man clambered up two more peaks, one with Martin at 900 metres and one with Martin and Thomas at 1010 metres. Another Pt 930 was accounted for twice, first by Martin who claimed to have walked and scrambled up it on his own, and then by Tom and Andy who skied up by a different route just to make sure. So, on the remote Northumberland Island in the far north of Greenland we had between us completed first ascents of nine peaks.

The solo ascent made by Martin was impressive, but it was also foolhardy. Wearing wellington boots and with no jacket and no equipment he was, or so I presumed, just going for a short Sunday afternoon stroll. Six hours later he had still not returned. 'Shall we go and try to spot him?' asked Tom and Andy. 'Yes, but take the VHF and keep in touch.' An hour later Tom radioed that they could see him in the distance, coming down a scree slope. He later claimed to have climbed Pt 930 metres, which was no mean feat in wellies and with no gear, particularly as there was some snow near the top. But I did also feel that it was irresponsible of him and dangerous to have gone off without a word and so ill equipped, and I said so. I am told that people with Asperger's often have little or no insight into how their behaviour affects others, but to me, Asperger's or not, in such challenging conditions his excursion put him and the rest of us at risk.

Passing time while we waited for Tom and Andy on their ski traverse we had come up with a new nautical term: 'floed out'. Huge fields of loose ice floes had been coming out of Smith Sound and were stretching right across to Canada. Sooner or later, at every anchorage we put into on the north coast of the island we had been invaded by ice floes brought in by wind or tide and had to move swiftly out, which was easier said than done. Hauling and winching anchors out from, and often stuck under, the floes was a chore until we invented a new technique which saved us a great deal of hard labour. Instead of anchoring we would motor out to a clear patch of sea and simply let the boat drift, with a watchkeeper on deck, until we came up to ice and had to move again.

After we had collected Tom and Andy from their traverse, we remained wind-bound in a favourite anchorage on the south coast, unable to land climbers. As a precaution we laid out the kedge as a second anchor. On the fourth night the wind rose to storm force. Someone tidying up on the foredeck, however, had removed the chain hook from the main anchor chain. In winds gusting to 50 knots the rope strop holding it parted, the rest of the chain shot out, and we were adrift. We ran before the wind, bare poled, while the lads struggled to haul in the trailing kedge anchor.

Later, as we were pushed farther south, 'What's the wind speed reading, Thomas?' I yelled. '53 knots,' came his reply.

Even under bare poles we had plenty of steerage way in those winds to allow us to steer past the next iceberg and bergy bit. Then we lay a-hull. By now the crew were all either feeling ill or being violently sick down below. The best I could do for them was to plug on under engine at about 60° to the wind and seas to try and reach Barden Bugt on the mainland for some shelter.

It took an age to come up to a big iceberg which I reckoned marked the halfway point near enough, and a further age to reach the far shore. By early morning we were close in, the storm had passed and the crew began to re-emerge, willing and able to take over from me. We found a more sheltered anchorage farther in than the one we had used in a storm in 2004, and in calm water and warm sunshine we chilled out for the rest of the morning.

Calm conditions prevailed and we returned that afternoon to our previous anchorage to retrieve the bower anchor. I wondered if we would be able to find it. As a last resort we could search by diving, but miraculously, on the first troll along the seabed with the kedge, Martin hooked the chain. All was forgiven. And I revoked my earlier private, critical thoughts about the 'pedants' glued to their GPSs watching the track of the boat as it veered around on her anchor in the storm: when the chain shot over the bow one of them had had the presence of mind to press 'mark' on his GPS. Gratefully we pulled in 80 metres of chain and motored ahead over the anchor to break it out from the sand.

At the end of August Tom and Andy left us at Qaanaq where Neil, who had suffered from post-traumatic stress disorder after a tour of duty in Bosnia, came out to join the crew. A keen and capable hand, he had some sailing experience under his belt. We now embarked on an interesting project and one that ranked high among the principal aims of our expedition: establishing the weather station on Littleton Island for SAMS and the Danish Space Agency.

To set up the station we would need to head still farther north, past Cape Alexander once more and into Smith Sound and Nares Strait where, now in serious and exposed territory, one feels vulnerable. Smith Sound is a main artery leading from the Arctic Ocean to the north and it is often subject to ice floating down to Baffin Bay. Indeed I heard later that one vast floe we observed had been measured from space and came in at a huge 3 kilometres long and 1 kilometre wide. However, because of the Coriolis effect and the way the earth spins on its axis, most of the ice tends towards the western side. We were able to squeeze up the eastern channel and find a relatively safe anchorage between Littleton Island and a smaller island to the north-west. We named the channel Dodge City because the current often brought down growlers and bergy bits which we had to push away with our *tuk*, or ice pole.

The station would contribute to ongoing research into Arctic weather patterns and the condition of the ice coming down from the Arctic Ocean. The instruments and batteries needed for the project were extremely heavy and had been weighing down the bows and altering the boat's trim, even across the Atlantic. But it did not seem to have affected the sailing too badly. Thomas and I now spent some time looking for possible sites. From email exchanges with SAMS, it became clear height was the most crucial factor so we chose an unobstructed site as high as possible on the south-west side of the island. Then came the labour of hauling all the gear up there.

Thomas, our 'mad scientist' – a retired science teacher – now came into his own, beavering away, drilling holes in the rock to anchor the triangular steel support poles (SAMS had supplied a huge drill), installing the equipment and setting up the electronics. He was helped by Neil and Martin, though the latter blithely suggested on the evening we had finished that the equipment might not have been aligned in precisely the right direction. I could see Thomas thinking, why didn't he say that before? Next morning they checked it out; all was well within the prescribed tolerances, transmitting information back to Scotland and Denmark from the moment it was switched on. The scientists were thrilled and the data was soon being shared via the internet. As a reward we broke open the excellent bottle of Bowmore whisky from Islay which SAMS had given us in anticipation.

We had another task on our list. The National Museum at Nuuk had asked us to seek any evidence of an ancient Inuit longhouse but although I searched the island high and low, I could find no trace.

Leaving Foulke Fjord a day or two later for the return on a fine calm morning, I was tempted to turn north to improve on 2004's 'farthest north of a production yacht in Greenland'. I am glad I was overruled. We had not gone far before a nasty depression caught up with us; the wind rose, a strong northerly with clag. Having set out for Upernavik we only made it as far as Northumberland Island. After a fortuitous rest on the Sabbath in a favourite anchorage on the north-west corner, we then enjoyed three days of following northerly winds under mainsail alone.

Six miles from Upernavik the wind increased rapidly to gale force, and backed round to the south. We were hit by our 'perfect storm' – well, as perfect as I ever want to encounter. I have been in stronger winds and bigger seas, but never for so long; this gale lasted two nights and a day. It was dark at night now, and misty, and there was ice about. We turned and ran before on bare poles, with the inner foresail flogging, caught somehow in a terrible tangle and unusable. When I tried the engine it would not fire up. So, bare poles, no engine, and there in the morning three icebergs standing in line to starboard towards which we were drifting. Unrolling a smidgen of genoa to give some slow steerage way, we slid past, not too close. We were now just able to head roughly north-westwards, away from the coast and icebergs coming out from the Upernavik Fjord and its glacier.

At the height of the gale, sailing fast under bare poles, Thomas, the mate, had suggested streaming warps to slow us. 'Are you sure about this?' I said. 'Come on, Bob, this is my life at stake here.' A strange collection of empty gas bottle, kedge anchor, chain and warp went over the stern. It did slow us down, but perhaps too much, making us less manoeuvrable. Soon he graciously admitted I had been right and we heaved it all back on board. My aft pulpit will never be the same again…

Next day conditions moderated slightly and we tried to beat back to make up the lost ground. We still had no engine; air must have entered the fuel lines. You cannot sail close to the wind on triple-reefed mainsail and a scrap of foresail, and the wind was directly from where we wanted to go, and increasing. We sailed as far as Kingigtortagdlit, an island some twenty miles from Upernavik with rocks all around it, but then gave up and hove-to again, this time on trysail and a bit of genoa, as the inner foresail was still in a tangle. During the night we lost 19 miles, again. The huge streaks of foam from breaking seas looked just like ice floes in the dark, and at times it seemed we were sailing across snow fields.

By morning the wind had at last decreased and veered and we could set sail for Upernavik, by now some forty miles away. The wind died almost to nothing and Martin did a fine job bleeding the fuel lines. We had just enough battery power left to start the engine which we revved hard, both to make sure it stayed running and to recharge the batteries. We motored full tilt for Upernavik.

By the time we reached harbour we hardly had a stitch of dry clothing left and as I was passing the hospital I thought they might have a room where we could at least dry our gear. The head nurse and doctor in charge came to our rescue. They called in staff (it was a Sunday), and not only dried out our clothes for us and allowed us to have showers, but they even gave us lunch. We were tremendously grateful.

While we were being made to feel human again Thomas ruefully confessed that the ice on these dark nights had really scared him; he also had building work at home that needed urgent attention. In short, he wanted to leave the boat. This was understandable, but it was going to make it more difficult for the rest of us sailing south and across the Atlantic, and he was concerned about that too. We worked out a compromise whereby he would stay on at least as far as Aasiaat, or even Nuuk, on condition that we stopped and anchored at night. Meanwhile, he would try and find a replacement.

Stopping at favourite anchorages each night, we headed southwards through the ice-strewn Vaigat Channel and across Disko Bay to Aasiaat. On 20 September, the day after we had arrived in Aasiaat, it snowed hard. Winter had come early to Greenland, and we still had a long way to go. Rather than attempt the North Atlantic in stormy conditions, I made the decision to leave the boat in Aasiaat for the winter.

This did not go down well with some of the crew. It meant extra expense with flights, and Neil especially was looking forward to his first Atlantic crossing, but it was getting rather late in the year. The boatyard in Aasiaat would haul us out on a cradle for a reasonable price. We stripped the boat and put everything in the yard's boat shed for the winter. After a few days' waiting – we learnt that some planes were out of commission for servicing at this time of year – we flew to Copenhagen and then home.

In spite of the aborted finale, it had been a successful expedition in the Tilman style and a personal renaissance, as it marked a new beginning after my years of enforced inaction, the result of the fire that destroyed the first *Dodo's Delight*.

The next summer's expedition was to be one of the happiest and most successful of all.

THE *IMPOSSIBLE WALL*

Never stop because you are afraid – you are never likely to be so wrong… Difficult is that which can be done at once; the impossible takes a little longer.

FRIDTJOF NANSEN, AS QUOTED IN *LISTENER*, 14 DEC 1939

They thought, or rather they cogitated, they came, they conquered.

JULIUS CAESAR (TRANSPOSED)

Some weeks after coming home from Aasiaat I received an email out of the blue from climbers I had never met: 'Bob, do you know of any big walls in Greenland?' They had climbed several big new routes on Mount Asgard in Baffin during the summer of 2009 and were keen to do some in Greenland in 2011.

I emailed back, 'I do know where there are some big walls in Greenland, but I am not going to tell you where they are!' (I wanted to save them for my own teams). 'But it so happens my boat is laid up in Greenland for the winter, so what about you coming this year?' They prevaricated, 'We'll have to think about that, and see whether we can raise the finance.' They could, and they did. I have always been hesitant about sailing with people whom I have never met. This might well promise to be the exception. They may not have been sailors, but they were world-class climbers; maybe they would prove to be as good on a boat as they were on a mountain.

That spring I returned to *Dodo's Delight*, in Aasiaat where I had left her the previous September, and prepared to relaunch her. Ferrying aboard the gear I had stashed in the yard's shed was hard work on my own. Furthermore, first the engine would not start and then the alternator would not work. A little ditty came to mind:

Sailing in Greenland without an engine
Is not nice
Because of the ice.

But surely the whalers and old shipmasters sailed engineless all the time, you will say. Yes, but remember many of them never came back; the best reason, I reckoned, for trying to get my engine working.

My international team comprised: Nico and Oli (brothers) and Sean, all Belgian (although Sean is also of Irish and Spanish extraction), and Ben, an American climber and a professional photographer. They had a reputation as being world class. Well, we would have to see. Owing to all the dancing, high fives and whooping that I had seen on their website on summiting, I had already dubbed them 'The Wild Bunch'. They enjoyed the joke.

They flew into Aasiaat and as they approached the boat I could see their minds working. 'What's it going to be like, for three months, in a small boat, cooped up with a crusty old Highland "priest?"' (They had a Catholic background – I usually think of myself as a minister.) In fact it worked out fine, and, as I am fond of telling people, it took them all of 10 minutes to realise that it was going to be fine: they saw that the skipper was used to living in exactly the same sort of mess as they were.

They had arrived on Greenland National Day and Frank, the manager of the boatyard, had invited us to the celebratory party. The team brought along their instruments – mandolin, concertina, tin whistle, bamboo flute and harmonica – and took over the party with music and song; the yard staff have never forgotten it. Next afternoon we went for a sail to learn the ropes as Ben and Sean had done virtually no sailing before, and the day after that we set off for Upernavik. The boatyard's engineer and I had fixed the engine, and the alternator seemed to be working. Little we knew.

There was not a breath of wind. We motored all the way across Disko Bay, again passing big icebergs that had calved off the glacier by Ilulissat to the east. Closing Disko Island, as we altered course to the north-west to begin the long haul round the west side of the island, the wind picked up, and the sea was flattish in the lee of land. We cut the engine and set sail. Icebergs loomed out of the mist at uncomfortably close quarters, and towards morning the wind died. We turned the key to fire up the engine. Not a peep. We tried again. Nothing. I was frightened of running down the batteries. There was nothing for it: we would have to complete the remaining miles to Upernavik under sail.

From then on it was slow going, and frustrating, particularly in dead calms, which are all too common because of the Greenland High over the ice cap. Afloat but going nowhere, one day Sean said, 'This must be the low point of the expedition.' As a Greenland veteran, I only hoped he was right and nothing worse would befall us. Then we felt a breeze, it strengthened, our sails filled and we tacked out. The sea became rough, a strong wind held right through the night and we put several brisk miles behind us before tacking to close the coast where, again, the wind deserted us.

Desperate to keep moving, Sean lowered himself over the stern and swam, trying to push *Dodo* through the water; I think he was joking, but progress had been woefully slow. Altogether it took us five days to complete what should have been a two and a half day passage. 'Well lads,' I said. 'You wanted to learn how to sail, didn't you?'

In Upernavik, we found that the engine problem was embarrassingly easy to solve. The cut off lever had been sticking. The alternator was still giving trouble. But these guys had come to climb, not hang around repairing boats. So hoping that the alternator would put at least something back into the batteries now the engine was running, and that the old wind generator at the stern of the boat might still be charging, I decided we should set off and climb.

Climbing: Upernavik area

We left Upernavik and motored the twenty-odd miles to the area of big walls that I knew about in the Sortehul Fjord. We studied *Impossible Wall*: I had been eyeing it up for a number of years but had never had a team strong enough, or willing enough, to attempt it. The lads asked whether there was anything else nearby that they could climb as a warm-up. We motored across the fjord to what I had dubbed *Red Wall*. As we drew nearer the team's enthusiasm became palpable; cracks and grooves stretched the full height of the cliff.

We anchored for the 'night' close to the old *rejsehus* (rest hut) in a shallow bay round the corner. In the morning we returned to *Red Wall* and the team identified the routes they would climb; two clear-cut dihedral and crack lines. As the wall dropped sheer into the water I could take the boat alongside, the men then stepped into the dinghy tied to the bow, and so on to the rock. First Sean and Oli, and then Nico and Ben. Before taking *Dodo* back to the anchorage

I motored around for a while, watching them and trying to video the action, but the camera they had given me was complicated for one so un-technically minded and so I had limited success.

While I waited in the anchorage I returned to the wall from time to time to see how they were getting on, but the wall was massive and try as I might I could not pick them out, even with binoculars. The climbers took some twenty hours to complete the two extreme rock climbs, one of 350 metres, the other of 400 metres, at E5 and E6 in climbing terms. They did them in one big push in continuous daylight. To save weight they had not taken the handheld VHF so I had no way of knowing when to go and fetch them from where they would walk off round the back. So when they completed their descent they had to walk all the way round the fjord behind the headland to the anchorage. The first I knew of their return was when Sean clambered aboard *Dodo* in the early hours and woke me up. He had stripped off ashore and dived into icy Greenlandic water. 'I needed the swim,' he said.

The team's next challenge was a dramatic wall in the Torssút, nearer Upernavik, which they had seen earlier. While they sorted out the mass of gear they would need for the climb on an industrial pontoon moored temporarily on the outside of the breakwater at Upernavik, I bought a portable generator. The generator was far too big and heavy for a small boat, and far too expensive, but it was the only one I could find, and if all else failed we would need it to recharge the batteries.

The cliff in the Torssút did not drop sheer into the sea, so this time there was no way to take *Dodo* alongside and we used the dinghy to ferry the climbers and their gear to the shore. I returned to Upernavik to try and solve our alternator problem while the team, after setting up a camp, would traverse in to climb the wall. So, I had plenty of time for my chore, and three or four days of investigation finally revealed that both the alternator and the spare were defunct. I had to buy a new one, at Danish-Greenlandic prices, but it was worth it as now the batteries would charge from the engine.

Knowing that the boat was in full working order may have lulled me into a false sense of security. The time came to pick up the climbers, and wanting to spare them a long dinghy ride, I anchored too close in and we took the ground when the tide went out. But that was fine: while we waited for the tide, the Wild Bunch played Tarzan, swinging out on the topping lift and dropping into the sea. Then as the tide returned they rowed out in the dinghy to lay a kedge anchor, and while one of them heaved on the winch the others jumped up and down on the bow to help shift the keel, I gunned the engine and we slid into deeper water. It was not the first time I have had to use this ploy.

Impossible Wall

The team's zenith was the first ascent of *Impossible Wall*. The route they chose was the steepest and the hardest, not only on the wall, but also probably in the entire area, and perhaps in all of Greenland: some 850 metres and nineteen pitches of sustained extreme climbing with no let-up. We put out fenders and took the boat directly alongside the wall, then moored with lines out fore and aft to climbing cams slotted into cracks on the granite face, the climbers stepped directly off the boat and on to the wall. The first crack line demanded a lot of 'gardening', and most of the grass and earth dislodged by the lads as they climbed landed on *Dodo*'s decks.

It took the team eleven days to complete the climb, with three portaledge encampments on the way. They had also packed their musical instruments in their haul bags and when bad weather caused a three-day delay they passed the time 'jamming' and composing new songs, suspended on the wall in their portaledges.

From time to time I would motor round and radio them for a progress report. Once when I asked how things were going I was told, 'Fine, Bob, yes, the acoustics are great.'

'Good, good,' I said. 'Glad you've got your priorities right. How's that other thing… what's it called now, oh yes, how is the climbing going?'

'The climbing? Oh yes, that's fine,' Sean said dismissively.

The chimney they called the 'black hole' was the team's next obstacle. After three days of rain it had become a wet, greasy slot, with water dripping continuously on the climbers. Sean, our loose rock, wet rock, grass, lichen, you name it, expert – nothing matters to him as long as he can keep on climbing – managed to lead the horrendous overhanging, wet chimney crack. And Nico, too, had his moments. The Greenlandic name (Timmiakulooq) for the wall means 'Seagull Cliff' or 'Bad Seagull Cliff', and it was. A fulmar Nico came upon guarding a ledge simply wasn't having it, and kept ejecting the foul smelling contents of its stomach over him. Once, as he tried to dislodge it, Nico had his mouth open… Finally, after repeated swings with a No. 4 cam, the fulmar relented and let him pass.

The team continued to make progress, climbing, hauling, filming, camping – and singing. In places, they found clumps of grass in the cracks and on the ledges, and a lot of banter between them came floating down, as in 'flowers for your Mum', together with lumps of sod. The *Wall* however had a sting in its tail: an unexpectedly hard penultimate pitch, overcome with a fantastic knee-lock by Nico to get it started – a technically difficult, and sometimes painful, manoeuvre whereby you jam your knee into a crack and use that as a lever to reach as high as you can to any possible holds above. This was especially remarkable as by that time Nico's stomach was ejecting its own contents forcibly and frequently: all four climbers had been collecting drinking water from the *Wall*, polluted by seabirds.

After eleven days, they topped out. They radioed the good news, 'We have climbed the *Impossible Wall*.' 'Ah, ce n'est pas impossible après tout,' I said, stretching my French to the limit. This time, I thought, they deserved to dance and whoop as much as they liked. They had climbed what was rated E7, 6c (British), or 5.12d (American), 850 metres. And now they would walk down the back of the mountain to the tents we had pitched before they started. For the team, the eleven-day climb seemed like only eight days. Able to make use of the continuous daylight they had climbed in stretches of 30 hours or more, and mainly 'overnight' when the sun would be shining on the west-facing wall. The next morning, leaving a little earlier than intended as a nearby iceberg had collapsed threatening to shed bits into the anchorage, I motored round to pick up the climbers. They rowed out to *Dodo*, we drank a champagne toast to *Impossible Wall*, and rejoiced.

'I think that must be the greatest adventure of my life so far,' Nico told me later. *Impossible Wall* was an astounding ascent, and I hope that it and other ground-breaking first ascents in the area reveal the tremendous potential for climbing at almost any standard here.

Aftermath and interlude

The climbers had overcome the 'impossible'. However a storm was forecast so we took an enforced rest in the only safe anchorage in the Sortehul, at its northern end. There we were joined by friends in their smart 55-foot Discovery *Saxon Blue*, on her way from Iceland, skippered by Rich of High Latitudes. I had known before I left Scotland that Rich would be in the area, but his arrival that day could not have been better timed. In the afternoon a group of kayakers from Wales, lead by Olly, whose group was to do another noteworthy route in this area two years later, also turned up and we all got together for a supper on *Saxon Blue*, for which my team naturally sang.

Indeed, music and song from the climbers was a feature of the expedition. In Upernavik they played and sang for Andrew and Maire, Royal Cruising Club friends, who were on their way to the Northwest Passage in *Young Larry*, and they performed again for a Swedish couple, Birgitta and Eric, and their crew on *Ariel IV*, also bound for the Northwest Passage, whom we met in the remote anchorage of Nuussuaq. Maire, a music teacher, also taught the team to play the spoons. Thereafter I kept finding bent spoons all around my boat, and Ben's endless practising nearly drove me crazy.

For me the hardest, but not impossible, challenge had been to disentangle a line which had caught around *Dodo*'s propeller… The climbers had been some distance from the top at the time so I told them I would be disappearing for a couple of days, looking for more big walls for future expeditions. I only found one, but I also found a beautiful remote keyhole anchorage. Weather and water were calm, so I attached a tripping line to the anchor, the seabed being an unknown quantity, and the floating line with its fender attached drifted astern and wrapped itself around the prop. Now, how was I going to get that free, all on my own?

Once before I had cleared the prop by getting the crew at the time to pull the boat close inshore, so that I could stand and then duck underneath without the need for an air bottle and all the diving gear. But here I had no crew. I did however have rocks. Twice, I nearly hit isolated rocks in deep fjords where the depth dropped from more than 100 metres to 4, 3, 2 metres in a matter of seconds. Were they volcanic towers? Or pingos? I have no idea. Whatever they were, they were in the wrong place on the charts. Or my boat was in the wrong place on the chartplotter.

I put the little outboard on the rubber dinghy, tied the dinghy alongside, pulled up the anchor, and motored dinghy and *Dodo* gently towards the shore with the 2HP engine. Then, I reasoned, I would stand on a rock, duck under the hull and clear the prop as before. But I could not reach to pull the zip across on the back of my dry suit. I tried attaching a line from the zip to a handle on the cuddy then strained and pulled backwards, but to no avail. In the end I had to duck underwater with the zip open. 'Bob, that's dangerous,' someone told me later when I mentioned it. And they were right. The weight of water trapped around my legs made it almost impossible to climb up the boarding ladder afterwards, but somehow I managed it and collapsed into the cockpit; and I had cleared the prop.

This excursion also prompted another make-do-and-mend incident. On one of my previous trips round to check out the climbers,

I had foolishly lost my smart Avon dinghy paddles overboard. This time I put in to Tasiusaq, a delightful bay fringed by a sandy beach, and rowed ashore with some wooden slats tied onto broom handles. On the beach I found some small bits of driftwood which would do as blades and some suitable lengths for handles, and made two paddles from the driftwood, which served us well for the remainder of the trip. When in Greenland, do as the Greenlanders do. The Inuit would have been proud of me.

Southwards

The lads next wanted to have a look at the climbing they had heard about at the southern end of Greenland. It was a long way, 850 miles, and there was either no wind, or 'it was in our faces' as one of them put it. We relied on the engine, diverting a couple of times up fjords where we had been told there might be big walls. In both cases they were not big enough for my team. In the second fjord, perhaps in frustration, the team stripped off and jumped into the water, whereupon Sean swam to an ice floe, clambered onto its small summit and sat there, stark naked, posing decorously like an artist's model. Stark raving…

A little farther south we spent a fraught evening avoiding growlers, bergy bits and bergs streaming out of a fjord with a glacier at its head. A day or two later we turned the corner of the aptly named Cape Desolation, eying up its cliffs as we went, and motored across the huge bay to the south to reach Nanortalik, the nearest main settlement to Cape Farewell, the southernmost tip of Greenland.

Nanortalik not only allowed us to replenish fuel and stores but also to study accounts of previous ascents left at the Tourist Office, from which we made our own notes. On putting out from Nanortalik a huge cruise ship was debouching its clientele into yellow launches to buzz them ashore. We hoped that Greenland and the Arctic would not go the way of Antarctica.

Cape Farewell area

Flanked by mountains, the fjords by Cape Farewell are beautiful and we were struck by how different they were to those at Upernavik, with their lofty sea cliffs. The whole area was much more Alpine in character, with well-defined peaks and ridges rising between the fjords. We turned in to the Torssukatak Fjord, where Oli got a ticking off for trying to sneak out some of the genoa and sail when we needed to keep motoring to maintain the course. The peaks of the Baron and Baroness passed to starboard, the sheer rock wall of the Thumbnail to port, and at the far northern end we turned in to Stordalens Havn and anchored. The bottom shelved rapidly from too deep for anchoring to a shallow silt bank, brought down by the river from the glaciers above. It took us more than one attempt to get our hook to hold. The bay was picturesque, surrounded by mountains and glaciers. Not surprisingly the lads made for dry land that evening to explore.

The next morning we returned down Torssukatak Fjord. Two of the team took cameras ashore and shot video of the boat with the Baron in the background. Just then a Frenchman I had met the year before in Aasiaat sailed through in his big steel boat on his way back to Nanortalik. He told us he had suffered some damage while at anchor one night and was returning for repairs. Farther down the fjord, close in on the west side, we dropped ours for the night, and the team prepared for climbing the next day.

Early the next morning it was misty as I rowed them and their gear ashore. I watched them walk away up the grassy slope and disappear. Somebody had to stay and look after the boat; besides, they were world-class climbers and I was not. They told me later that they had got lost, only stumbling on their chosen peak when the mist chanced to lift. World-class climbers do not carry compasses? Whatever their map reading skills, they had climbed 'two classic, clean, direct crack lines on excellent rock', as Nico described them afterwards. We named them *Condensed Milk* and *Corned Beef*, two of the skipper's favourite foods. This late in the year, August, the nights were drawing in so they had reached the summit in the dark, enduring what they were pleased to call a 'shiver bivy' at the top.

In the early morning light next day they had traversed the challenging ridge to the eastern subsidiary peak, before abseiling down and making their way back to the valley. The views all around had been quite stunning, they told me. From the valley it had been a 5-kilometre trek back to where *Dodo* and I were waiting. I felt very honoured when they told me they had named the main peak *Shepton Spire*, a play on the well-known *Shipton Spire* in the Himalayas. We returned to the anchorage at Stordalens Havn.

Exploring fjords farther east, we examined and rejected various options, but noted one strong possibility on Quvnerit Island. But the lads were very keen that I should do a climb with them. We passed a wall that didn't look too forbidding, and I agreed to give it a go. However, as Nico pointed out later, there were a couple of flaws in the plan. To begin with, it turned out to be 500 metres of climbing rather than 200 metres. And then from up past an overhang a voice came down to me: 'Er, Bob, I think this is a little harder than we originally thought.' And they were absolutely right. Not only did I take a long time to surmount the overhang, and that with a bit of kindly help from Sean, but moving up a crack line later I got my foot irretrievably stuck in the crack. Heave, push, turn: it just would not come out. At last, 20 minutes later, it somehow fell out. 'OK Bob, that's right. Now move across to the right.' A pause. 'Er… Sean, the other foot's stuck now.' Eventually I did arrive at the top, completely shattered. It was far too long and far too hard a climb for an old man, however expertly guided. For days afterwards my arms were so stiff I had to invent a pulley system to lever them up to grasp the handle for heaving myself out of my bunk. But hey, I had become a fully paid-up member of the Wild Bunch, dancing and yelling like the best of them there at the top!

An early start next morning just as the sun was coming up, and the others began their walk in to the inviting wall we had noticed on Quvnerit Island. While they were hard at it, I spent most of the day resting on the boat. From a distance the wall appeared to have finger cracks, but when they got closer, they found they were really off-width cracks, awkward things to climb at the best of times, and they had left their bigger cams behind. Despite this they started up two hard, long direct lines. High up, Nico took a fall. He had climbed some eight metres above Ben on the belay and lacking suitable cams had put in no protection. He had grasped a sizeable block above with both hands to make the next move, and the block started to come away from the face. A split second later he had to let it go and take the fall, ending up suspended 8 metres or more below Ben, upside down and facing a 400-metre void below. Considerably shaken, he climbed back up to Ben and they pressed on. 'I think you must have been praying for me,' Nico said when he got back. 'Of course,' I replied.

Ben was also pretty shaken. The falling block had, almost miraculously, missed his head, bouncing off the face above him. But what had made the deep graze on his ankle? And why had he later found the pocket knife in his rucksack broken in two, if not by a chunk of projected rock?

Both climbing pairs met at the top in the evening, and enjoyed, or rather suffered, another 'shiver bivy'. The next morning they traversed the entire length of the ridge, taking in a couple of peaks on the way. But they did not claim these as first ascents, as they had found some tat (old gear) on their way. But they had added another two new extreme climbs to their tally, both at E5, 550 metres.

After all this excitement we retired to the nearby settlement of Aappilattoq, on the way passing a Danish hydrographic survey vessel. We had rafted alongside them at Nanortalik and got to know them a little, and now over the radio we told them about one or two suspected rocky patches in the fjords from which we had recently returned. They seemed glad to have something specific to investigate. The harbour of Aappilattoq is gained via a narrow channel between rocks. While we were there a motorboat manned by a crew of missionaries came in. Ben was an atheist and sceptical of all religion, whereas I was intrigued and took names and addresses, although I have yet to follow them up. Some children from the settlement came on board and were fascinated by the gang's musical instruments. The lads tried to teach them how to play them, but with limited success.

At Igdlorsuit, a bay at the entrance to the final fjord, Prinz Christian Sund, we found another big wall, just as the weather closed in. There was no climbing to be had that day, which may have been just as well: Nico was still shaken from his fall. Instead they set themselves tricky climbing challenges in the valley floor on big boulders that may have fallen from the wall, or perhaps been brought down and left when the glacier receded. Altogether they had still made five major first ascents of hard climbs in the Cape Farewell area.

Atlantic again

Prinz Christian Sund was our gateway to the Atlantic. And the last chance for any treats: I knew from the past that the weather station at the far end usually had delicious Danish pastries. We were not disappointed. The lads wanted to sail the Atlantic 'for the experience'. They were not disappointed either. I couldn't resist saying before we departed, 'We should be in Scotland in twelve days' time – or dead!', and indeed it turned out to be a fast and gale-strewn passage, for we were into September by now. Post-tropical storm Danielle had also been tracking along by Nova Scotia and Newfoundland so we did not turn south but kept along the parallel of 61°N.

There was high pressure over Scandinavia, Britain and Europe and the depressions could not get through to the east, so we found ourselves endlessly making long ocean tacks along this parallel of latitude, against strong easterly winds for several days. Danielle then had the cheek to turn north and spin up past us, trailing in her skirts heavy line squalls accompanied by the banshee shrieking of wind in the rigging. We hove-to under trysail and backed storm sail – the inner foresail rolled to a storm jib – to let it pass. Later two depressions joined together and became quite vigorous, and we had to heave-to again. In all we hove-to four times. Maybe I tend to heave-to earlier these days. The shock as the boat falls off a wave, followed by an explosion like an artillery gun going off as it lands in the trough below, is something I tend to avoid if possible. I was secretly pleased that the gang were impressed: one night I heard Ben saying, 'At least Bob knows when to stop.' Having said that, the last time we hove-to was to give us a break in calm conditions, in order to tighten the nut holding on the wheel, controlling the steering cables.

When we were at last able to alter course southwards the westerlies promised by the weather faxes proved to be a long time coming. Eventually a following wind did materialise, bowling us along on a broad reach or run, goosewinged, with mainsail and poled-out genoa on opposite sides, towards Scotland, the only casualty being the bookcase which fell off the bulkhead and crashed to the floor narrowly missing Ben's legs in the bunk below.

Off the Rockall bank we had a close encounter with a big fishing trawler, but with so many deck lights showing it was hard to pick out its navigation lights. Eventually we made out both port and starboard lights at the same time and knew we must be crossing its bows. They flashed us with a searchlight so we fired up the engine just in case but continued sailing, and soon we saw them pass safely astern.

The Mediterranean sailors among us always seemed to be in a hurry, calling for more sail, whereas the skipper was often minded to roll in some genoa, or reef the mainsail, and it was under full mainsail and rolled genoa that Mingulay and Berneray, the two most southerly islands of the Outer Hebrides, at last appeared dead ahead. And there, off a sandy beach on the east side of Mingulay, we anchored for the night, surrounded by a huge colony of seals lining the waterline and moving up and down with the tide.

Next morning overruling the idea of attempting a climb here – 'it would be cool to climb on both sides of the Atlantic' – as the weather forecast looked threatening, we ran across the Minch, past the Cairns of Coll, and anchored for a second night in Loch Drumbuie opposite

Tobermory. Then down the Sound of Mull the next day. As we passed Duart Castle and out into the Firth of Lorne towards Oban we were met with a full gale. A fine homecoming… Had this perhaps something to do with this being my thirteenth Atlantic crossing, the date being the thirteenth of the month, or the large number thirteen for some unknown reason stitched on to my trysail? No, no, we were not superstitious…

For our efforts we were awarded a Piolet d'Or; the golden ice axe is one of the world's most prestigious mountaineering awards. The citation was for what they called our 'Greenland Big Walls' expedition, climbing nine new routes on the big walls on the west and south coasts of Greenland of which 'the most committing route' took eleven days. After we collected our golden axe the Wild Bunch, still on the stage, gave an impromptu concert – of course. Next day over in Courmayeur for another presentation the mayor actually invited them to play and sing in the main square, with the local mountain guides in traditional dress standing behind us. It's never a quiet life with the Wild Bunch.

08

A GRAND FINALE

Although there have been articles in sailing and climbing magazines and specialist journals about our voyage through the Northwest Passage, it seems appropriate to end this book with a fuller account of the passage, offered as a finale to the book but not, I hope, to my adventures. As I approach my eightieth year these can only become more challenging.

THE NORTHWEST PASSAGE

Come my friends,
'Tis not too late to seek a newer world.
Push off ... for my purpose holds
To sail beyond the sunset, and the baths
Of all the western stars, until I die.
It may be that the gulfs will wash us down:
It may be we shall touch the Happy Isles...

ULYSSES, ALFRED, LORD TENNYSON

Until recently whenever anyone asked me, 'What about the Northwest Passage?', I would tell them I reckoned it would be irresponsible to attempt it in a comparatively small glassfibre boat like mine. This feeling was strengthened by hearing of an American in a larger glassfibre boat than mine who only succeeded at his third attempt, and had to be rescued by an icebreaker on one of the attempts. But recently conditions, on average – although you can never be certain from one year to the next exactly what will happen – have improved. So when in 2012 a crew of strong South African climbers who were looking for adventure expressed a keenness to do it, I agreed to give it a try. I also had my own reasons.

Earlier there had been a chance of joining Cristina in her superyacht *Billy Budd* for the passage. It was Cristina who had employed me the year before in the Arctic and I had written an article in *Yachting World*, telling the story of the trip and attempting to assess the advantages and disadvantages of superyachts in comparison to small boats like mine. By the time the editors had done their stuff, and the more humorous asides had been cut out, although not intended that way, the article might have come over as being rather critical. As a result, Cristina and her skipper Clive thought it best not to employ me (Cristina in her kindly way has forgotten all about that now and we are the best of friends). So if I was going to do it, it would have to be in my own boat.

The Northwest Passage isn't particularly beautiful – in fact the landscape is fairly flat and if not barren at least unproductive and largely uninhabited. There was little likelihood of any climbing along its length. So why did I want to sail it? We are back to the main motive of these adventures: it was the challenge. Though conditions have been improving in recent years, it is still one of the rites of passage for the adventurous. Conditions cannot be guaranteed from one year to the next, there is ice, and it is always possible you might not make it. There are dangers and risks to be surmounted, and very few fibreglass boats have done it. So it had to be done – if we could summon the courage.

Three South Africans – Steve, Andy and Clinton – stepped off the bus at the Glencoe crossroads and stayed on the boat. Steve was the leader of the gang but all were young, fit, lean and strong climbers. *Dodo* was rather cheekily tied up against the pontoon at the Marine Resource Centre at Barcaldine, not something that is usually allowed. We bought vast quantities of food, and stowed this and the climbing gear as best we could round the boat. We took pictures of ourselves in the smart jackets Gore-tex USA had sent us to test as part of their Shipton-Tilman Award and went for a trial sail, as two of the crew had done little sailing before. We also practised rigging the trysail in case we hit stormy weather. We were ready to go.

We left Barcaldine on the west coast of Scotland on 8 June, stopping briefly in Dallens Bay round the corner to pick up the Royal Cruising Club burgee which I had left behind, a terrible mistake. Steve was keen to press on, but that evening we anchored off the ruins of Ardtornish Castle in the Sound of Mull, Somerled's main base in his wars against the Vikings, then took our departure next day through the Sound of Pabbay. For several days we enjoyed steady north and north-easterly winds, unusual in this part of the Atlantic, and bowled along at a great rate. At one stage, sailing with a favourable wind on a sunny day, Andy turned to me with a smile and said 'So, Bob, is this your gale alley?'

'Well,' I countered, 'I knew if you had thought it was going to be easy you wouldn't have come.'

When fair breezes began to fluctuate we motored or sailed until a south-westerly slant drove us north-westwards. What was different about this passage from the ones that had preceded it, now that *Dodo* was on her way north once again? This time, over 1700 miles and thirteen days later, at 0200 one misty morning we came upon a huge band of concentrated pack ice that must have stretched some 60 miles out from Nanortalik and Cape Farewell. We had arrived at the south coast of Greenland. The silent, unfriendly pack stretched as far as the eye could see. In the half-light we turned tail and motored south-westwards before a favourable wind allowed us to sail west and north, eventually to round Cape Desolation, giving it a good berth in case of ice, and so towards Paamiut. We were short of diesel by then, but by motoring at low revs managed to eke it out, and reached Paamiut without running dry, passing the strange large wreck still perched upright near the shore to starboard. It had been a varied but good passage.

If the crew of 2010 were the 'Wild Bunch', this lot were the 'Nerdy Bunch'; I have never had a crew who spent so much time on their computers. In Paamiut the Dane in charge of the diesel station lent us a house where we could shower, wash our clothes, and where they could spend hours at their computers. To keep in trim physically they also found some rocks for bouldering nearby.

We were due to pick up another South African climber, Dave, at Aasiaat. After provisioning we put to sea. This time I was struck by just how long the west coast of Greenland appears to be when you are plugging by in a small boat at 5 knots or so. It seemed to go on forever. Perhaps I am getting old! There was no wind, and we had to motor almost the whole way – as I have said before, in Greenland there is either too much wind or too little, and we had too little most of the time. We also stopped as little as possible. But we did divert to the superbly protected Irkens Havn, the 'Tinkers Hole' of the west coast of Greenland, to change the engine oil. Next morning, quite unaware that we had swung right round in the night, I tried to leave through a rocky sill at the opposite end of the hurricane hole, over which the tide was ebbing fast, rather than the channel we had come in by the day before. Frantic reversing under full power saved the day. It was near here in a previous year that I had chanced upon that ancient Inuit cemetery where many of the graves, which could only be rocks piled up in this barren land, had broken open, displaying the skulls and skeletons within.

Approaching Hamborgeland the wind strengthened and began to head us so we took the inner passage. As we navigated through this scenic route we passed a number of tantalising, unclimbed cliffs. 'It's like a kid looking through the window of a locked candy store,' Clinton remarked as we, reluctantly, left them behind.

Sisimiut is a favourite harbour of mine: well protected, quite small, the downside of that being that it becomes crowded with bigger fishing boats and local dories with powerful outboard engines. We provisioned, and the crew made good use of the Wi-Fi at the Seamen's Mission. We also needed to buy a rifle. You are unlikely to encounter polar bears on the west coast of Greenland except perhaps in the far north, but you almost certainly will in the Canadian Arctic and along the Northwest Passage, and they can be unpredictable and highly dangerous. The Canadians practically insist that you have a gun, and I knew there was a shop in Sisimiut that sold them second hand.

The rifle shop was up the hill to the right of the Seamen's Mission. For the sake of Steve, who was making a film of the expedition, I had to repeat coming in and asking for a rifle so he could film it. The owner entered into the spirit of it all too. In all we bought the same rifle three times. Soon after leaving Sisimiut, some five miles out, I test fired it at an iceberg but it failed to eject the cartridge, even after frantic bolt action. There was nothing for it but to go all the way back and return to the shopkeeper, who replaced it like for like without a murmur and gave us an extra box of shells for our trouble. The next test was successful.

At Aasiaat we picked up Dave, our fourth South African, and headed towards Upernavik. My climbing team and crew now comprised: Clinton, perhaps the best-known climber in South Africa; Andy, ever-helpful and a talented climber; Dave, who was a more cautious climber than the others, which was no bad thing, and a very experienced sailor, which was a very good thing; and Steve, another talented climber who had recruited and organised the group in the first place. I have to say I did find Steve rather pushy – he always wanted to be pressing on rather than any stopping or pausing. He was also something of a healthy-eating addict and while our diet appalled him, I am afraid we carried on as usual.

Naked iceberg climbing seemed to amuse our South Africans for some reason. Choosing a suitable looking berg in Disko Bay, they stripped down and paddled across in the dinghy and in the nude with no crampons and only one ice axe each they claimed a first ascent, raising the South African flag on the summit before swimming back to the boat, leaving one of them to row the dinghy back. A strange South African custom? Shock tactics to acclimatise for those used to warmer climes? Or simply madness? I shall never know. Whatever, when we reached the Sortehul Fjord near Upernavik we set about investigating some 'proper' climbing.

Climbing

The team decided, as the Belgian/American team had done in 2010, to warm up with some new routes on *Red Wall* on the east side of Agparssuit, a challenging playground of potential new routes. We anchored round the corner and during the night another yacht slipped in to anchor nearby – an unusual occurrence in Greenland. Next morning when we went back to *Red Wall* there was a young man in a dinghy from this yacht who told us he was counting the sea birds on the cliff, and would we please not climb there. I wished him luck, looking up at the thousands of sea birds wheeling, soaring, diving round the cliff, and making a tremendous din. So we moved away and thought no more of it, assuming he had meant in the immediate area where he was. Months later I received an official-looking letter stating that he had meant the whole cliff, and complaining that we had ignored his instructions. Fortuitous perhaps that we had misunderstood, but not intentional.

Further round on the east side of the headland I tried to lay the boat directly alongside the cliff, but the swell was too great and the team had to land by dinghy, pulling it up behind them onto the ledge. They climbed two new routes here. Climbers have a habit of giving strange names to their climbs and the first they called *Don't be Gull-able,* an E3, 5.10d, C1, 6a (British), 300 metres, and the second they named *Flight of the Dodo* an E4, 5.11d, 6a, 400 metres. *Flight of the Dodo* was an especially gratifying route, sustained and direct. I was a little disappointed that Andy had not gone back to climb the roof free (redpointing climbers call it) i.e. without using the gear for handholds

– a more purist way to climb – but he had his reasons, maybe thinking of Dave, his second.

The wind changed direction so I decided to move the boat to the other side of where the promontory narrowed. Andy and Dave, while walking down from the top that evening, saw the boat and came down to the beach. Clinton and Steve on the other hand did not, and walked right round the fjord to where we had been anchored the night before. Tight rock shoes that have to fit your feet like a glove are so excruciatingly painful especially when walking that Steve had taken his off, and had clambered over the boulders barefoot, his feet bound only with climbing tape. The boat with the bird man on board, which was still anchored where we had been, gave them a lift round to us on their way to Upernavik, just as we were about to pick up our own anchor to go and look for them.

After a brief rest and much sorting of food, water and gear the team were ready for their main task: another big route on *Impossible Wall*. For me there was something of a disappointment here. I had hoped they would tackle a series of diagonal overhanging corner cracks well away and different in style from the pioneering Belgian/American route of 2010. But they thought there might be a blank section halfway up which might stop them, so instead they chose a complementary route, close to and similar to that original route. It was, however, a fine route in its own right; sustained, technical, and challenging at E6, 5.12b, 6b (British), 850 metres and took them nine days, sleeping occasionally on portaledges. They finished up the top two pitches of the previous route, which was fair enough as it was on the direct line of their own route. In my mind though this fine effort would always be overshadowed by the Belgian/American route, in European and possibly US climbing circles too, but it made them heroes in South Africa.

While they were on the wall, and hearing via the VHF radio that they were likely to be there for some days, I took the boat off to Upernavik. The electric anchor winch had stopped working, and there was trouble with the batteries. The climbers suddenly woke up to the fact that they were now completely on their own. When we met up again they mentioned this, and it did make me wonder if I had been right in leaving them to their own devices. But then I thought climbers in Greenland would normally have to hire a fishing boat, at vast expense, to drop them off, and arrange a date for their collection. By having a boat at their disposal my team were, I felt, rather lucky, nay spoilt, even if they did have to fend for themselves for a few days.

Back at Upernavik for rest and recovery the boat disappeared under a blanket of equipment: sleeping bags airing, climbing gear, tents and drying clothes. The crew were impatient to leave but Cristina was due to fly out to *Billy Budd* which had been sailed there by her professional skipper and crew, and I had been invited to dinner four days hence. It would have been impolite to refuse such an invitation, the food would be a treat, and in any case I looked forward to meeting up with them all again. I wasn't disappointed: fine food, pleasant craic and a delight to meet up with the guests, some of whom I already knew, and the new crew.

My crew didn't miss out on all the feasting either. We all enjoyed a tremendous meal with my friends Jens and Rasmine in their house near the top of the settlement. The lads, never backward in coming forward, had made some remark like, 'it would be really interesting to know what Greenlanders used to eat in the old days.' Jens and Rasmine took them up on it, and the meal consisted solely of a variety of the foods eaten by the Inuit in the past: whale, seal – raw and cooked – narwhal, musk ox, even down to a small dried fish which, according to my friends, was the main reason the Inuit had been able to survive towards the end of the winter when all other food had gone. It was quite an experience, and a great evening.

The morning after the dinner we started out on the four-day crossing to Pond Inlet on north Baffin. The aim was to find new routes in that area of fjords 40 miles south-west of the Pond Inlet settlement I had visited before. After some time searching we found what we were looking for in White Bay – a series of impressive, unclimbed white cliffs, with their own miniature 'Half Dome', reminiscent of Yosemite National Park in the USA. Dave had been stretched on the big wall and elected to stay with me on the boat, but Andy, Clinton and Steve left in high spirits and with equally high expectations. They soon discovered however that the fine-looking cracks we had seen from a distance were 'blind', and would take no cams and chocks to protect them. They were forced to go round the corner to an area with more features, and they put up a new route at a slightly lower grade, which they aptly named *Bonfire of the Vanities* at E3, 5.11a, 6a, 280 metres. But great stuff; it was a pioneering route, the first ever on a series of completely unclimbed cliffs in an area of huge possibility, if the problem of protection can be solved, and hopefully without recourse to artificial means or bolts.

Into the ice

Pond Inlet is an open roadstead and shallow, not ideal for replenishing a boat. Everything had to be carried out some distance by rubber dinghy including the fuel in containers. Navy Board Inlet, one of the possible entrances to Lancaster Sound and the Northwest Passage, was full of ice, while a curious long arm of concentrated ice stretched several miles out into Baffin Bay from the north-eastern corner of Bylot Island, and the wind was from the east, so we were effectively blocked from starting the Northwest Passage. We later met an Italian boat, *Best Explorer*, who had attempted the passage eastwards round Bylot Island; a large dent in their steel hull bore witness to the fact that we had made the right decision to wait. But it was frustrating.

After five days the internet ice charts we had been studying in the library showed signs that the ice might be dispersing. We left Pond Inlet there and then, and hammered hard under power for Navy Board Inlet. In 24-hour daylight we negotiated 2/10ths ice through to Tay Bay at the far end and anchored precariously off the big glacial estuary fan to ferry water across to the boat in our 15-litre containers – it was quite a difficult exercise in the lively conditions, but we had been told the water in Pond Inlet gave people upset stomachs. We were careful to take the rifle we had bought in Greenland ashore, as I had seen a polar bear here once before. Next day we made our way across Lancaster Sound, seeing no ice in spite of the predictions, to Dundas Harbour, where we anchored again for the night in the south-east corner where, although it was a lee shore, I knew the depth was sufficiently shallow for anchoring.

A cruise ship arrived next morning, fortunately just as we were leaving. And so started a long hard slog under engine the length of Lancaster Sound against a relentless west wind. One night, we put in to one of the many inlets on the northern shore for a rest, although it was a struggle to find anywhere shallow enough to drop anchor off the incredibly steep-to shoreline. The next evening a Canadian Coastguard vessel asked us to shift outside of themselves as they were surveying the seabed and had to keep a steady course. We complied, and both vessels headed for Terror and Erebus Bay by Beechey Island, the Canadians to continue their survey within the bay, *Dodo*'s crew to look for the graves from the 1845 Franklin expedition in which Captain Sir John Franklin and 128 men perished.

It took us a while to find the right site and as we searched we were not impressed by the amount of detritus which had been left by later expeditions. The three graves from Franklin's two ships date from when he had wintered here – the deaths were probably due to lead poisoning from the food tins. A French expedition was camped at the site, researching the life of Joseph René Bellot (1826–1853), a French lieutenant on one of the British ships that had been sent to find Franklin. He had given his name to the Bellot Strait farther south. Bellot had drowned later after falling through a crack in the ice pack, and they had obtained permission to dedicate the fourth, unmarked, grave to his memory, and told us all about it, filming as they talked.

The passage from Beechey Island proved taxing. A strong south-westerly drove us north-westwards, well reefed down, but we could not make the corner and south coast of Cornwallis Island in order to reach Resolute. When close in to land the wind headed us and we had to use the engine to push us round and along the south coast, and finally for the approach to Resolute. We had some trouble with the shallow waters here but in the end dropped our anchor off the west shore to get some protection from the wind. *Billy Budd*, which we had seen anchored here in the distance, must have left in the night after refuelling without noticing us.

Both Resolute's main hotel and the fuel distribution system are owned by one man, the Australian known locally as Ozzy. The fuel lorry comes down to the shore, and the hose has to be ferried across the water by dinghy to boats anchored as close in as possible. Even large yachts like Cristina's had to do it this way, and in lively conditions, which I maintained served them right for taking on 7000 litres as opposed to our tank of 150 litres.

We left Resolute the next morning in a snow storm, and a strong north wind sped us down towards Peel Sound. The boat rolled and crashed southwards and the snow did not make for pleasant watchkeeping, but I had a tough crew. The ice that had been blocking the entrance had receded by the time we got there, which allowed us to sail into and down the Sound. But unfortunately the beluga whales which *Billy Budd* had reported sighting previously had also departed. It took us two days to reach False Strait just north of the famous Bellot Strait, which cuts off Somerset Island from the Boothia peninsula, the most northerly point of the mainland American continent. Here we discovered an unrecorded and well-protected anchorage in Leask Cove. That evening the lads went off to look for musk oxen, successfully, and polar bears, unsuccessfully. During the night the crew of *Nordwind* (whom we had first met at Resolute) must have passed by the cove without seeing us. We saw them anchored at the far end of False Strait the next day.

The charts depicted heavy concentrations of ice farther south between King William Island and the Boothia peninsula. We had no internet access on the boat, so you may wonder how we were getting ice charts at all. Mike Anderson, my son David's business partner in Ballachulish back in Scotland, would download the relevant Canadian ice chart and chop and compress it small enough for us to receive as an attachment to an email via the sat phone. It was an idea we had got from John Harries of Attainable Adventures, and it worked well.

Both *Nordwind* and *Dodo* decided next morning to traverse the Bellot Strait 'for fun'. The Strait has something of a reputation: both boats got the tides wrong and struggled at Magpie Rock where the Strait narrows and the tidal current rushes through at a fearful rate, but eventually we made it to Fort Ross, a former outpost of the Hudson Bay Company, and anchored in the wide bay. We had been told that this was polar bear country, but look as we might we never saw one.

Several ships had over-wintered here in years gone by and one of the two remaining buildings was still in good repair, stocked with some provisions in case of emergency. The Hudson Bay Company had established the station in 1937 but only manned it for eleven years as it became uneconomical to run. We added our boat's name to those written on one of the walls. But the bottle of wine that *Billy Budd* had left for us had been 'stolen' by another boat – a heinous crime in such a 'dry' land! Next day both skippers got the tides wrong, again, and by Magpie Rock we came to a standstill in spite of full revs; we could not stem the flow, but *Nordwind*'s more powerful engine inched her through. We followed a few hours later but, to the dismay of my crew, missed the two polar bears *Nordwind* told us they had spotted and watched for a while in the Strait.

A band of pack ice blocked the far western end of Bellot Strait, but we were able to bypass it by going close to the shore. We continued south in clear water for a couple of days until heavy ice forced us to turn back. We found *Nordwind* where they had told us they would be, anchored in the Tasmanian Islands, and dropped our hook nearby. It was as well that we did: that night a strong gale blew up from the east. We were anchored close inshore with plenty of chain out but *Nordwind*, more exposed, lost her bower anchor and close to 90 metres of chain. And then, while ranging about in the night, the clamp bolts holding her prop shaft to the gearbox flange had loosened, allowing the shaft to shift back a little. The German owner who was on board gave Alex, the professional skipper, a hard time for not having put a retaining strop on the anchor chain and insisted they make a systematic search for the anchor and chain, which were original to this classic 86-foot wooden yawl. (*Nordwind* had been built for the German Navy in 1939, requisitioned by the Allies in 1945 as a Windfall yacht, and lovingly restored at huge expense by the new owner.) We offered to help with the search by lending our kedge anchor so it could be dragged along the seabed, and also tried to help with securing the prop shaft, using some makeshift bolts. It was at this stage that Richard Haworth arrived aboard the rather luxurious motor yacht *Boethuk* on which he was acting as ice pilot, and he also offered his help, diving to look for the anchor, which was hidden in dense kelp. Unfortunately he had to abandon this when the regulator he was using from *Nordwind* froze.

Some three days later the prop shaft was repaired enough for the engine to be run at 1000 revs, but the search for the anchor and chain had to be abandoned, and both boats continued south. Another sailing boat we met heading west to east gave us advice on the ice status in Victoria Strait, which was a tremendous help. It was very unusual for the strait to be open for small boats – it was where Franklin's two ships became trapped and eventually lost – and we seized the opportunity. Not having to go via Gjoa Haven with its difficult, shallow channels to the north and south would save us several days. So after a while we crossed over to Cape Felix on the north-west corner of King William Island, and along the shallow west coast of the island, dropping our anchor temporarily close in to change the engine oil. En route we passed a large, white Russian cruise ship at anchor in the mist, which at first we took to be a big iceberg, and so over towards Jenny Lind Island. There was, however, ice in Icebreaker Channel to the north of this so we detoured the extra miles round to the south, and on to Cambridge Bay. *Nordwind* had been following the edge of the pack ice all the way through, but had a difficult night threading through the floes in Icebreaker Channel in thick mist. By taking this channel they did however arrive in Cambridge Bay before us. We were now, at least psychologically, halfway through the Northwest Passage, having completed the most difficult part. But there was still a long way to go.

Out of the ice – and into the Smoking Hills

Sometimes the moments that challenge us the most, define us.
DEENA KASTOR IN *SPIRIT OF THE MARATHON*, 2007

Apart from some sharp practice by the fuel company – three boats rafted together were each charged $157 for an out-of-hours call-out from the same fuel lorry on the same visit – and the painfully slow Wi-Fi at the local hotel, Cambridge Bay was welcoming. Having gone the long way round via Gjoa Haven, where Amundsen had spent two winters, Rich arrived that afternoon and invited me aboard *Boethuk* for a good chat.

Being in harbour we were also in maintenance mode. So coming over to *Dodo* later, Rich cleverly joined the cable from the masthead VHF antenna, which we had been forced to renew, to the coax cable below. Andy had by this stage already begun the job of changing the fuel filters fairly frequently, as we had experienced an alarming hiccup in the flow of the fuel by Jenny Lind Island. Clinton meanwhile had taken on the role of topping up the diesel tank from the containers kept on deck – everywhere we could we bought more to make sure we had enough to reach the next settlement, which could be as far as 700 miles away, if there was no wind. Clinton had no trouble picking up the heavy 20-litre containers and carrying them to the cockpit, whether at sea or alongside. However, topping up at sea involved putting a large funnel in the intake pipe to the tank and using a tube to siphon out the diesel until the container was light enough for us to lift and pour the rest of the fuel directly into the tank. Not the easiest of jobs at sea.

Dave was adept at using electronic navigational systems, some of the more advanced being new to me. I particularly appreciated the way he was careful not to try and take over as skipper; he would sometimes make suggestions, but waited for me to make the final decision. Steve continued as our conscience, dietary and otherwise, but we took little notice. Corned beef (sometimes) and porridge (every day) were still on the menu. And they all stood their watches without demur whatever the conditions, conscientiously hand-steering whether sailing or motoring.

In Cambridge Bay we renewed some stores, bought a Canadian gas bottle – yet another gas system to add to the plethora of different fittings and screw threads – and that evening some of the crew went to explore the wreck of Amundsen's old *Maud* (as opposed to his *Gjoa* which is on display ashore in Oslo). The *Maud* had lain in the harbour for over eighty years and was recently subject to a bid from Norway to bring her home – something to which the residents, who have become rather attached to their famous relic, are strongly opposed.

Our main concern now was the distance involved in reaching Point Barrow and crossing the Chukchi Sea down to the Bering Strait, nearly 2000 miles farther on. Enjoying fair winds we made good progress down the Dease Strait, anchoring in shallow water off Lady Franklin Point. At this point I felt I needed a rest; old age again! The next morning the helmsman drove us hard into a rock. On his own admittance he had not been watching the echo sounder closely enough. We pulled up the floorboards and could see no damage, and motored on into the Dolphin and Union Strait. Towards evening I ordered a diversion into Bernard Harbour, the site of an old Distant Early Warning station. Here we lifted the floorboards again and, being calm and at anchor, we sponged out the bilge and made a thorough inspection. Thankfully we could still see no water ingress or damage and concluded that we were safe to carry on. Nevertheless I decided to stay the night as we were tucked into harbour. The lads took the opportunity to go ashore, but they still saw no polar bears.

Dolphin and Union Strait and Amundsen Gulf go on a long way and our passage was not helped by a westerly headwind into which we made wide tacks under sail to avoid slamming into the waves. Westerly cruising boats are not good to windward and we made little progress. When we came abreast of Cape Parry the wind veered more into the north-west and we were able to head towards the Bathurst promontory. Closing the shoreline we had to turn north again and it became a hard bash on the engine along this barren coastline. We had intended to go through the shallow Snowgoose Pass by the Smoking Hills (they do literally: deposits of lignite – shale and sulphur together – ignite spontaneously when they become exposed to the air, and have done so for centuries), but in those seas there was no way we could risk that. We continued to battle on in increasing seas until we rounded Baillie Island to the north and turned south-westwards. A little more off the wind now, we could thankfully shape a course, turn off the engine and sail towards Cape Dalhousie and Tuktoyaktuk, better known as 'Tuk'.

Off the Mackenzie River delta the waters are incredibly shallow. Sailing with 2 metres or less under the keel for miles on end is a nerve-wracking experience. The channel into Tuk is buoyed, but is of no greater depth, and we were surprised to see a large tugboat ahead, obviously shallow of draught and specially designed for working in these waters. At the industrial dock, normally out of bounds to yachts, the tug, *Kelly-O*, indicated we should tie up alongside her. We were immensely grateful to be offered showers and given a square meal after such a long and hard passage.

We spent nine days in Tuk, but by this time we had moved to the Town Quay. Gales in the Beaufort Sea to the north were predicted on the GRIB charts we were accessing on the neighbouring yacht *Marguerite*, and indeed when the gales did come they took a good swipe at Tuk as they swept past. The lads found a guest house owner who allowed them to use the Wi-Fi and let Steve edit his film. Spending hours on shore editing was fine, but Steve also insisted on editing while we were on passage. I never knew making a film took so many hours; the Wild Bunch of 2010 had made an excellent film, *Vertical Sailing*, but they had edited all their footage at home.

During this second half of the voyage, small frictions between skipper and crew surfaced. Dave and Steve were old friends, but as

Steve had married an American and now lived mainly in the USA they had not seen much of each other recently and they had a lot of catching up to do. But to me it sounded like an endless machine gun-like staccato, back and forth for hours on end without a break. In the small confines of a boat it became increasingly annoying, at least to me. After about an hour I would ask them politely if they wouldn't mind continuing their discussion on deck, and my sanity would be restored. Five people with different lifestyles, living together in close proximity, on a boat, for several months at a time, calls for compromise and forbearance.

Tuktoyaktuk's communal deep freeze is a system of tunnels and chambers dug into the permafrost. We were taken down the long wooden ladder and had a good look round with our head torches, although it seemed to be more of a tourist attraction nowadays, not used so much by the local community. I also went to church, an informal Pentecostal service in which young people, together with adults of the community and their pastor, played guitars and sang.

To make the most of the daylight hours, and to help us avoid any logs brought down from the Mackenzie River, we set out early. As Steve and I got up we were apprehensive. The sound of wind in the rigging was constant, but time was pressing. After a long haul north-westwards to pass Hooper Island we were able to turn into deeper water, where a favourable wind invited us to scupper our plans of visiting Herschel Island – known to be a favourite haunt of polar bears – and the possible anchorages of Demarcation Point and Brownlow Island. Unfortunately the wind then went west again and strengthened, and we began to struggle, tacking and bashing against the seas and wind. When we eventually tacked back again we found we had made limited progress down the course line. But by the next morning the wind and sea had moderated and we put the motor back on and made our way up to and then entered the shallow lagoon to the north-east of Barrow. We navigated through this for some seven miles inside the line of islands, watching the echosounder closely all the while in these shallow depths before finally putting our anchor down at the top north-west corner in 1.1 metres of water under the keel. At least there was little tide and the depth remained fairly constant. We waited here for an extra day and night as a favourable east wind was forecast for the next leg. The crew had not been cleared into America yet, and as they had seen a few US-plated 4x4s cruising around, after some debate among themselves they finally decided not to go ashore to look around.

As we got up to go the following morning, Steve remarked that with the strong winds forecast, if I thought it was better to stay another day because of the winds he would be quite happy with that. I appreciated this coming from Steve, but I told him that I thought staying here in 40 knots of wind with only 1.1 metres of depth under the keel might be more dangerous than meeting it outside. We made our way out through the break in the reef, and past Point Barrow. Officially, some say, we had then completed the Northwest Passage.

This was however, by no means the end of the story. There are virtually no suitable anchorages down this part of Alaska's west coast and a gale was forecast. Only one place might give shelter – Peard Bay, an anchorage behind Seagull Island, some fifty miles south of Barrow. But it didn't look that friendly on the chart and the wind was from the north, so we gave it a miss and kept going. The wind increased, the seas built and it was certainly a ferocious and unpleasant day and night of gale force winds in shallow seas, but we did make rapid progress running before under bare poles. Trying to sleep in the night, I heard a big wave bang hard against the side of the hull and pencils, log book, charts and perhaps even the computer shot off the chart table and crashed to the floor. We left them where they were and slept on fitfully.

The next day the wind moderated until strong winds again caught up with us on a shallow stretch of water some fifty miles north of the Bering Strait, where the seas were extremely confused. An involuntary gybe ripped the mainsail almost in two, luckily just below the second reef so we could still use it. We sailed on and as we approached and passed through the Bering Strait that night things became quite benign. The next morning we were beam and broad reaching, in sunshine at last, and bowled along the coast, making Nome that evening. Entering the small boat harbour, Rolland, who was to become our contact man, directed us to a berth. We tied up alongside a Swedish sailing boat, *Anna,* and when all was squared away, we reflected on what we had achieved. The crew had come through with flying colours. I shook them all warmly by the hand. We had braved the Northwest Passage.

Postscript

Our intention had been to go on down to the Aleutian Islands and winter the boat somewhere there. But the climbers were keen to return home. Dave had to get back to South Africa for work, then Steve left a day or two later, with his film completed. We had arrived in Nome on 20 September, late in the year this far north, and the harbour was expected to ice over by mid-October. Andy and Clinton stayed on long enough to help me try to get the boat hauled ashore, but a strong northerly had driven too much water out of the harbour. They left, and a week later I succeeded in getting *Dodo* onto Rolland and fisherman Phil's trailer, then towed by a 4x4 to a compound. Rolland built a cradle around her, and there I left her snugged up for the winter.

It had been a successful expedition and I was exhausted: 6059 miles from Barcaldine, Scotland, to Nome, Alaska, and 2860 miles from Pond Inlet through the Northwest Passage to Nome. The team had proved themselves to be first-class climbers and pretty good sailors, too. Especially as two of them had done virtually no sailing before; the Atlantic, the west coast of Greenland, and the Northwest Passage is not a bad way to start.

It seems best to end the book here on this high, though hopefully the adventures are not over yet...

GLOSSARY

This is not intended to insult the initiated – it may be helpful for those who enjoy adventure but are not too familiar with sailing terms and boats, and also climbing terminology.

SAILING

amidships middle section of a boat.

bow front end of a boat.

port left. Port wine is red and the port-hand navigation buoys are red – this side of the Atlantic. The Americans like to be different and have them the other way round!

starboard right. The Viking boats were steered by a steering oar mounted at the stern on the right side of their ships, and the term remains – steerboard, right side.

stern aft end of a boat.

Anchoring

bower anchor main anchor of a boat. Usually stowed on a bow roller at the bow.

kedge anchor second, usually lighter, anchor, sometimes put out in addition to the bower in stormy weather.

tripping line line attached to the front of an anchor so that if it gets jammed in some way on the seabed it can be 'tripped' – pulled up from the front rather than by the chain attached at the back end.

Points of sailing

beam reach wind at about 90° to the boat.

beating (*see* close hauled)

broad reach at about 120° to the boat.

close hauled sailing as close to the wind as possible, with the sheets and sails hard in.

close reach with the wind at about 60° to the boat. Faster and more comfortable.

goosewinged sails out on opposite sides of the boat to catch as much wind as possible when running before.

on the wind (*see* close hauled)

running before sailing with wind astern

Rigging

stays or shrouds the wires attached to and holding up the mast.

aft lowers shrouds going to halfway up the mast to stop it 'panting' – flexing back and forth, and side to side.

backstays wire(s) to the aft end of the boat, from the masthead.

cap shrouds wires to the top, or near the top of the mast to give it lateral stability.

forestays wires at the bow end of the boat, in front of the mast, supporting the mast.

halyards the lines that haul up the sails (hauling on yards – cross timbers – in the old sailing boats).

sheets the lines that control the sails – their shape, how much they are hauled in tight or let out.

truck fitting at the top of the mast to which the shrouds are attached.

Sails

genoa large foresail set on the first forestay.

jibs smaller foresails, sometimes on an inner forestay.

leech aft end of sail.

luff front end of a sail.

mainsail main sail of the boat, attached to the mast and the boom at its foot.

trysail small storm mainsail.

yankee blade shaped foresail.

Storm tactics

heaving-to way of stopping the boat, and drifting slowly downwind. The jib is backed against the wind, the reefed mainsail or trysail let out the other side and the wheel or tiller put right over. All are working against each other and stopping the boat.

lying a-hull lying across the waves with 'bare poles' – no sails up.

running before in extreme conditions running before the wind and seas, often with no sails up (bare poles).

trailing warps long ropes trailed behind the boat in a loop to slow the boat down when running before in a storm.

CLIMBING AND SKI MOUNTAINEERING

belays stances or places where it is possible to stop and attach oneself to the cliff, in order to safeguard the other person climbing by taking in the rope as he climbs, or paying out if he is leading.

crampons metal plates strapped underneath boots with forward and downward spikes which allow climbing on and up ice.

crevasses splits or fissures in the surface of glaciers or snow slopes, sometimes deep and sometimes wide, and often dangerous.

'gear' or protection cams or chocks which can be placed in cracks, or slings round blocks or projections, which allow the main climbing ropes to be put through an attached carabiner (snap link), so that if the leader falls he only falls to the chock (and the same distance below) before being stopped. It provides some protection against the dangers of falling.

harscheisen 'crampons' for skis.

jumars implements with teeth that slide up a rope but grip on a downward pull. Some have built in hand grips and by attaching oneself to it, it is possible then to 'jumar' up the rope. Alternatively a thin line can be used with special knots which slide up the rope but resist downward pressure.

pitches sections between belays.

Features

col the dip or depression between two hills.

lateral moraine the debris (rock and earth) carried down and pushed to the sides by a glacier.

terminal moraine the debris carried down to the foot of a glacier.

pingos mounds formed in the Arctic by layers of ice building beneath the surface and pushing the earth or seabed up into a hill or mound.

Smoking Hills on the south-eastern side of the Bathurst peninsula sulphur rich shale (lignite) ignites naturally when exposed to the air. Believed to have been burning for centuries.

Equipment

tuk Inuit word for a wooden pole with a metal blade used for testing the ice before walking on it, or for pushing ice away by sailors (longer pole).